Naval Records
for
Genealogists

N A M Rodger

PRO Publications

PRO Publications
Kew
Richmond
Surrey TW9 4DU

Crown Copyright 1998

First published by HMSO 1988
Previously issued by the Public Record Office 1984

ISBN 1 873 162 58 8

A catalogue card for this book
is available from the British Library

Contents

List of Tables

Foreword to the Third Edition

This edition follows the arrangement of its predecessors, but incorporates a number of corrections, and adds records which have been transferred to the Public Record Office since 1988.

List of Illustrations

CHAPTER ONE

Introduction

Scope

This book is intended as guide to the official records of the Royal Navy of England, later of Great Britain, now in the Public Record Office which are concerned wholly or largely with named individual officers or ratings. Virtually all records contain some references to people by name which might be of value to the genealogist, but this guide is concerned only with service or personnel records. It does not include private or unofficial documents, archives not in the PRO, records not yet transferred from the Ministry of Defence, published works, Royal Marine service records or medieval and Tudor records (of which only fragments survive).

The naval service records in the Public Record Office present the enquirer with a number of difficulties. The arrangement of the archives in groups and classes does not correspond closely to the original organisation of the documents by the administrations which created them. The lists appear in many cases to have been drawn up by persons unsure of the origins or the nature of the documents they refer to, and are consequently confusing to the searcher. The titles of the various ranks and ratings which have been used in the Navy are often unfamiliar to enquirers, and are not always correctly used in the lists. Finally, neither the Admiralty or the PRO has ever evolved a consistent terminology for the record themselves, so that it is difficult to tell from the lists what exactly the documents contain. For all these reasons the seeker after information on individuals who served in the Royal Navy is often perplexed, many searches are fruitless which need not be, and many of the records, including some of the most valuable, are seldom used. This little book is intended to improve that situation, and to enlighten the task of the social historian, or the genealogist using the Public Record Office in search of naval ancestors.

Arrangement

There is no chance of explaining the naval service records without first explaining whom they refer to and how. Chapter Two describes the structure of the ranks and ratings in the Royal Navy from the seventeenth century to the twentieth in sufficient detail to enable the enquirer to follow a naval career and to understand the arrangement of the records. It does not attempt even to sketch a general social history of the Service. Chapter Three establishes a classification of naval personnel records into thirty-two standard types, which are used consistently throughout this book in each of the baffling variety of terms used both in the records themselves and in PRO Lists.

The records defined in Chapter Three are mostly those kept by, or on behalf of the central administration of the Navy, that is to say by departments of the Admiralty, or by the subordinate bodies which until 1832 transacted much of the administration of the Navy; the Navy Board, Victualling Board, Sick and Hurt Board, and Transport Board. Until 1853, however, none of these bodies kept records of naval ratings, almost all of whom were recruited, both in law and in fact, not to the Service as a whole but to a particular ship for a single commission. The only service records for ratings, and an important series for officers, were therefore the Musters and Pay Books kept by individual ships. These books are numerous (there are about a quarter of a million of them), complex, and very unlike the personnel records produced by naval administration ashore, and they have been treated separately, in detail, in Chapter IV.

The records other than Musters and Pay Books are so varied and fragmentary that they are best described in a tabular form. This has been done in Appendix I, which lists all the naval service records in the PRO, Musters and Pay Books alone excepted, under the standard headings established in Chapter Three. The tables set out the ranks or ratings described by the record, the dates it covers, brief remarks if appropriate, and a series, if any, to which it is assigned in Appendix II. The entries in Appendix I are the only mention in this book of all known naval personnel records in the PRO, and the reader seeking further information about the contents of those not listed in Appendix II must consult the PRO Lists.

In Appendix II have been assembled all those records which survive in their original series as created by the naval administration, or in substantial fragments of these series. Because these archival units do not often correspond to PRO classes, they have described in a neutral terminology ('Series A', 'Series B' etc), as dissimilar as possible to either Public Record Office or Admiralty usage. These 'series' are established solely for the explanatory purposes of this book, and only the PRO references can be used for ordering documents in the Search Rooms.

In some cases two or more discrete series of records were bound together in volumes, but later transferred to other classes and replaced with different records. In these cases each type of record has been treated as a series regardless of the other series with which it may from time to time have shared a volume, so that a single 'piece' (the item ordered by a single PRO reference) may include parts of several series, and individual series may run over several PRO classes, or even groups. (See for example Series AX and BF)

Each series in Appendix II is provided with a brief introductory note outlining its provenance and contents, and all those records which are included in the series have their series reference noted in Appendix I, so that only the unrelated fragments, not capable of being assembled into series, appear in Appendix I alone.

The personnel records of the Royal Navy include those of many auxiliary or quasi-naval organizations such as the naval reserves, all of which are described briefly in Appendix III.

Records Elsewhere

Naval personnel records are in principle transferred to the PRO when they are seventy-five years old, or the persons concerned are dead. At present the service records of ratings entering the Navy from 1892, and of officers entering from various dates between 1890 and 1907, are held by the Ministry of Defence CS(R)2E, Bourne Avenue, Hayes, Middlesex. They are not open to public inspection. Certain records of later dates have however been transferred to the PRO and are noted at appropriate points in this book, which also takes the definitions and descriptions in Chapters Two and Three up to 1945.

Navy List

This book deals only with unpublished documents, but there is one published source so fundamentally important that it must be mentioned. The official *Navy List*, published continually from 1814, contains a great deal of information of value to the historian and genealogist, and is the natural starting point of any search for an officer's career in the nineteenth and twentieth centuries. It contains seniority lists of officers which are keyed to lists of ships of the Navy with the officers appointed to them.

In its original form the *Navy List* included seniority and disposition lists of all commissioned officers, Masters, Pursers, Surgeons, Chaplains, Yard officers, and officers serving in the Coast Guard, Revenue Cruisers and packets. The following were later added:

1838	Naval Instructors
1842	Mates (later Sub-Lieutenants)
1852	Chief Engineers
1862	RNR Officers
1870	Boatswains, Gunners, Carpenters, Assistant Engineers, Midshipmen, Navigating Midshipmen, Naval Cadets, Navigating Cadets

1884	Head Nursing Sisters
1888	Head Schoolmasters
1890	All other warrant and commissioned warrant ranks

During the two World Wars, much of the usual information was omitted from the published editions of the *Navy List* and confined to Confidential Editions for Service use only. These Confidential Editions have been transferred to the Public Record Office as a record class (ADM 177) and are consequently included in this book. They are not generally available elsewhere, but the ordinary (in peace time complete) editions of the *Navy List* may be found in many libraries. There is a complete set available in the Public Record Office.

CHAPTER TWO

Ranks and Ratings

Introduction

Nowadays, even a expert can be fairly precise about what is meant by a naval officer and a naval rating. Although there remain some anomalies in both cases, the lines between officer and rating, and between officer and civilian, can be drawn with some accuracy. All officers today hold rank, and with one exception take rank, by commission.

This straightforward position has existed for less than forty years. From the seventeenth century to the twentieth the officers of the Navy fell into several overlapping and often ill-defined groups, not all clearly distinct from ratings. The most senior, and before the nineteenth century the most easily defined, were the commissioned officers ('commission officers' in the old form). They consisted originally of the various ranks of Admiral and Commodore (collectively known as flag officers) Captains and Lieutenants. These ranks were at various dates increased by the addition of Commanders, Lieutenant-Commanders and Sub-lieutenants, and by the transfer or promotion of warrant officers to commissioned rank. With limited exceptions among small and non-combatant vessels all HM Ships have always been commanded by commissioned officers.

Beneath the commissioned officers came the warrant officers, a disparate group; some whose history was more ancient than commissioned officers and their status scarcely inferior, others who had the standing of petty officers and were distinguished from them only by being appointed by warrant rather than rated by their captains. By the eighteenth century, however, a conventional distinction was drawn between those warrant officers who, like the commissioned officers, were reckoned as 'sea officers' and those who were only 'inferior officers'. Sea officers, whether commissioned or warrant, were officers in the usual modern sense, persons exercising a general authority aboard ship. 'Sea officer' in the seventeenth and eighteenth centuries therefore corresponded to the modern 'naval officer', which then referred only to the civilian, shore-based officials of the Navy Board, and never to the officers of the Navy.

Warrant sea officers were the heads of specialised technical branches of the ship's company for which they were responsible to the captain directly. For purposes of keeping accounts and drawing stores they answered to one of the administrative boards which governed naval affairs. They were in many cases examined professionally, or served an apprenticeship. The bodies responsible in the eighteenth century for examining, warranting and keeping account of various warrant officers can be set out in Table 1. Those above the line are sea officers, responsible as indicated for their accounts; those below it (plus the Surgeon's Mates) were inferior officers and kept no accounts.

Table 1 Warrant Officers, 18th Century

Officer	Examined by	Warranted by	Responsible to
Master	Trinity House	Navy Board	Navy Board
Surgeon (& Mates)	Barber-Surgeons' Company (from 1745 Surgeons' Company). From 1796 Sick and Hurt Board	Navy Board (from 1796 Sick and Hurt Board)	Sick and Hurt Board
Purser	-	Admiralty	Victualling Board
Boatswain	-	Admiralty	Navy Board
Gunner	Ordnance Board	Ordnance Board	Ordnance Board
Carpenter	apprenticeship	Admiralty	Navy Board
Cook	-	Admiralty (from 1704 Navy Board)	-
Chaplain	Bishop of London	Admiralty	-
Armourer	Ordnance Board	Ordnance Board	-
Schoolmaster	Trinity House	Admiralty	-
Master at Arms	-	Admiralty	-
Sailmaker	apprenticeship	Navy Board	-

Among the warrant officers the Boatswain, Cook, Purser, Gunner and Carpenter were distinguished as 'standing officers', in principle warranted to a ship for her lifetime regardless of whether she were in commission or not. When their ship was in reserve they were borne on the Ordinary books of the dockyard, and were supposed to employ themselves aboard in the maintenance of the ship,

In the table above the warranting authorities for the different warrant officers are given, but both warrants and commissions (normally given by the Admiralty) could also be issued by Commanders in Chief overseas. Subject to confirmation, these commission and warrants were good, and conferred seniority just as those issued at home. If the necessary examinations could not be arranged locally, acting commissions or warrants were issued, confirmable on passing at the first opportunity. In circumstances when their orders did not allow them to issue commissions or warrants, flag and commanding officers could appoint officers to fill vacancies by orders, which carried no seniority, and no pretentions to a confirmed commission or warrant. Certain inferior officers were also appointed by order from the Admiralty.

The relative position of commissioned and warrant officers was transformed during the nineteenth century by the transferring of many of the warrant officers to commissioned rank, and the creation of the new branch of Engineers, first as warrant officers, then partly by order and partly commissioned, and finally all commissioned officers. This complicated the hitherto simple distinction between the commissioned officers who fought and commanded the ship, and the warrant officers in charge of specialist branches, who had no claim to command. It then became necessary to distinguish between commissioned officers of what were called the Military and Civil Branches, or in modern parlance between executive and non-executive officers. These distinctions applied both to commissioned and warrant offices and maybe set out in Table 2, as they existed in the nineteenth century:

Table 2 *Military and Civil Officers, 19th Century*

Military	Civil
Commissioned:	*Commissioned:*
Admirals	Surgeons (from 1843)
Commodores	Pursers (from 1843)
Captains	Chaplains (from 1843)
Commanders	Engineers (from 1847)
Lieutenants	Naval Instructors (from 1861)
Mates/Sub-Lieutenants	
Masters (from 1808)	
Warrant:	*Warrant:*
Boatswains	Engineers (1837-1847)
Gunners	Carpenters (from 1878)
Carpenters (to 1878)	

It will be seen that from 1847 only three warrant ranks remained after the transfer to commissioned rank of all the other branches. In practice this development was largely complete much earlier, for in 1808 (the year Masters were ranked with Lieutenants),

Pursers and Surgeons were raised to 'wardroom rank', which meant that they too were for all practical purposes treated as though they were commissioned officers.

Later in the century, the position was again complicated by a quite different process whereby individual officers were given the opportunity to advance to commissioned rank. At the same time the pace of technical change was leading to the creation of new specialist rating branches ineligible for promotion to Boatswain, Gunner or Carpenter. New warrant ranks were therefore created for these branches, which in turn became eligible for promotion to commissioned rank, so that the three warrant branches of 1847 to 1867 had by 1945 become twenty-four (plus others in the RNR and Coast Guard), of which all but one could proceed to commissioned rank. This process is set out in Table 3, covering 1865 to 1945, giving the dates of establishment of each rank and subsequent changes of name. Note that these are dates of establishment; first promotions were not necessarily made until years later, while on the other hand some initial promotees received seniority back-dated to before the creation of the rank. Some of these ranks had very few holders in their entire history, or only one or two at a time. The table is not intended as an accurate guide to relative rank, but in general commissioned warrant officers ranked with but after executive officers of equivalent rank.

The inferior, later 'subordinate' officers of the eighteenth and early nineteenth centuries include two distinct categories. Among them were persons appointed by warrant from the Admiralty or other boards - and hence warrant officers - who were not counted as sea officers, and had the social and professional standing only of petty officers. They were the Surgeon's Mates, Armourer, Cook, Master-at-Arms, Sailmaker, Chaplain and Schoolmaster. From 1790 Caulkers and Ropemakers, recruited from the dockyards, were warranted by the Navy Board, and later Coopers, who had formally been ratings, were added.

The other inferior officers were the Midshipmen and Master's Mates. Though in principle petty officers rated by the Captain, they were recognised as potential sea officers, with the all-important social distinctions of being permitted 'to walk the quarter deck', and to wear uniform, and in practice their position was quite distinct from and superior to that of other petty officers.

Besides the categories already noted (commissioned, warrant, inferior, petty and standing officers) one other is sometimes met with in the eighteenth century, signing officers. This refers to four officers who signed the ship's books: Captain, Master, Boatswain and Purser.

Table 3 *Commissioned Warrant Officers*

Petty Officer's Rating	Warrant Rank	Sub-Lieutenant	Lieutenant	Lieutenant-Commander	Commander	Remarks
Boatswain's Mate Chief Petty Officer	Boatswain	Chief Boatswain (1865) Commissioned Boatswain (1920)	Lieutenant (1903)	Lieutenant (1903) Lieut.-Cdr. (1914)	Commander (1918)	Hon. Lieutenant on retirement (1887)
Gunner's Mate Chief Petty Officer	Gunner	Chief Gunner (1865) Commissioned Gunner (1920)	Lieutenant (1903)	Lieutenant (1903) Lieut.-Cdr. (1914)	Commander (1918)	Including Gunner (T) from 1880. Hon. Lieutenant on retirement (1887)
Carpenter's Mate Chief Shipwright (1918)	Carpenter Warrant Shipwright (1918)	Chief Carpenter (1865) Commissioned Shipwright (1918)	Carpenter Lieutenant (1903) Shipwright Lieutenant (1918)	Carpenter Lieutenant (1903) Carpenter Lieut.-Cdr. (1914) Shipwright Lieut.-Cdr. (1918)	Shipwright Commander (1918)	Relative rank of Lieutenant on retirement (1887)
Schoolmaster (to 1919)	Headmaster (1867) Head Schoolmaster (1889) Schoolmaster (1919)	Chief Schoolmaster (1904) Schoolmaster/Senior Master (1919)	Headmaster (1920) Headmaster Lieutenant (1937)	Headmaster (1927) Headmaster Lieut.-Cdr. (1937)	Headmaster (1929) Headmaster Cdr. (1937)	Headmaster (1867) originally a rating equivalent to warrant rank. From 1919 rating branch abolished and entries made directly to warrant rank.
Chief Engine Room Artificer	Artificer Engineer (1897) Warrant Engineer (1920)	Chief Artificer Engineer (1903) Commissioned Engineer (1920)	Engineer Lieutenant (1903) Lieutenant (E) (1926)	Engineer Lieutenant (1903) Engineer Lieut.-Cdr. (1914) Lieut.-Cdr. (E) (1926)	Engineer Cdr. (1918) Commander (E) (1926)	Promotion from ERA to Mate (E) to Engineer Lieutenant/ Lieutenant (E) was possible 1912-1931. Warrant Engineer (1903 ff) and Chief Warrant Engineer (1916-1920) were RNR equivalents.

(continued)

(continued)

Sick Berth CPO Wardmaster	Head Wardmaster (1900) Warrant Wardmaster (1916)	Commissioned Wardmaster (1916)	Wardmaster Lieutenant (1918)	Wardmaster Lieut. Cdr. (1921)		
Chief Yeoman of Signals	Signal Boatswain (1902)	Chief Signal Boatswain (1902) Commissioned Signal Boatswain (1920)	Lieutenant (1903) Signal Lieutenant (1918)	Lieutenant (1903) Lieut.-Cdr. (1914) Signal Lieut.-Cdr. (1918)	Signal Commander (1918)	Before 1902 listed with Boatswains.
Master at Arms	Chief Master at Arms (1910) Warrant Master at Arms (1920)	Commissioned Master at Arms (1917)	Lieutenant at Arms (1918)	Lieut.-Cdr at Arms (1918)		
CPO Telegraphist	Warrant Telegraphist (1910)	Commissioned Telegraphist (1910)	Telegraphist Lieutenant (1910)	Telegraphist Lieut.-Cdr. (1918)		
Chief Stoker Chief Mechanician	Warrant Mechanician (1910)	Commissioned Mechanician (1910)	Engineer Lieutenant (1917) Lieutenant (E) (1926)	Engineer Lieut.-Cdr. (1917) Lieut.-Cdr (E) (1926)	Engineer Cdr. (1918) Commander (E) (1926)	
CPO Writer	Warrant Writer (1910) Warrant Writer Officer (1944)	Commissioned Writer (1915) Commissioned Writer Officer (1944)	Assistant Paymaster (1917) Paymaster (1918) Paymaster Lieutenant (1918)	Paymaster (1917) Paymaster Lieut.-Cdr. (1918)		
Ship's Steward Victualling CPO (1917) Supply CPO (1922)	Head Steward (1910) Warrant Steward (1915) Warrant Victualling Officer (1920) Warrant Supply Officer (1922) Warrant Stores Officer (1944)	Commissioned Steward (1915) Commissioned Victualling Officer (1920) Commissioned Supply Officer (1922) Commissioned Stores Officer (1944)	Assistant Paymaster (1917) Paymaster (1918) Paymaster Lieutenant (1918) Paymaster Lieutenant (V) (1920) Paymaster Lieutenant (1922)	Paymaster Lieut.-Cdr. (1918) Paymaster Lieut.-Cdr. (V) (1920) Paymaster Lieut.-Cdr. (1922)		

(continued)

(continued)

CPO Cook	Instructor in Cookery (1910) Warrant Instructor in Cookery (1918) Warrant Cook (1931) Warrant Cookery Officer (1944)	Commissioned Instructor in Cookery (1918) Commissioned Cook (1931) Commissioned Cookery Officer (1944)	Lieutenant Instructor in Cookery (1920) Paymaster Lieutenant (1931)	Lieut.-Cdr. Instructor in Cookery (1928) Paymaster Lieut.-Cdr. (1931)	
Chief Armourer	Warrant Armourer (1911)	Commissioned Armourer (1916)			Entries ceased 1919, most transferring to Ordnance Branch.
Chief Electrical Artificer	Warrant Electrician (1911)	Commissioned Electrician (1911)	Electrical Lieutenant (1920)	Electricial Lieut. Cdr. (1921)	
PO or Second Hand	Skipper (1911)	Chief Skipper (1916)	Skipper Lieutenant (1935)		RNR Trawler Section or Patrol Service only.
Chief Ordnance Artificer (1919)	Warrant Ordnance Officer (1919)	Commissioned Ordnance Officer (1919)	Ordnance Lieutenant (1919)	Ordnance Lieutenant Cdr. (1919)	Branch established 1919.
Officers' Chief Steward	Warrant Steward (1934) Warrant Catering Officer (1944)	Commissioned Steward (1934) Commissioned Catering Officer (1944)			Paymaster-Lieutenant (OS) on retirement.
CPO Photographer	Warrant Photographer (1937)	Commissioned Photographer (1940)			
CPO Airman	Warrant Observer (1938) Warrant Air Officer (O) (1943)	Commissioned Observer (1938)	Lieutenant (A) (1938)	Lieut.-Cdr. (A) (1938)	Fleet Air Arm.

(continued)

(continued)

CPO Airman	Warrant Air Gunner (1939) Warrant Air Officer (AG) (1943)	Commissioned Air Gunner (1939)	Lieutenant (A) (1939)	Lieut.-Cdr (A) (1939)	Fleet Air Arm.
Chief Air Artificer	Warrant Aircraft Officer (1939)	Commissioned Aircraft Officer (1939)	Lieutenant (E) (1939)	Lieut.-Cdr. (E) (1939)	Fleet Air Arm.
Chief Air Mechanic	Warrant Air Mechanic (1939)	Commissioned Air Mechanic (1939)	Lieutenant (E) (1939)	Lieut.-Cdr (E) (1939)	Fleet Air Arm.
CPO Airman	Warrant Pilot (1940) Warrant Air Officer (P) (1944) Warrant Pilot (1945)	Commissioned Pilot (1940)	Lieutenant (A) (1940)	Lieut.-Cdr. (A) (1940)	Fleet Air Arm.
PO	Boom Skipper (1940)	Chief Boom Skipper (1940)			RNR Boom Defence Service only.
Chief Stoker	Boom Engineer (1940)				RNR Boom Defence Service only.
CPO	Warrant Recruiter (1942)				Same rank existed in RM

Beneath the officers of all sorts comes the mass of what in the eighteenth century were known as 'the people', or 'private men'. All were ratings, that is rated by their captains to a position which was both 'rank' and job. During the nineteenth century, and particularly after the introduction of Continuous Service in 1853, a distinction began to be made between a permanent or substantive rating, which conferred a standing in the Navy as a whole analogous to an officer's rank, and could be altered by the captain only in specified circumstances, and a 'non-substantive' rating which represented the actual job performed by the rating, with the standing conferred by it on shipboard, which might be higher than that of the substantive rating. Though a captain's liberty to rate or disrate is nowadays limited, the distinction between substantive and non-substantive ratings still obtains. Both, but especially the latter, are still a combination of job and status, each dependant on the other.

Officers' Ranks

Flag Officers

In the organisation of the Navy in the mid-seventeenth century there was only a single battlefleet to which major warships belonged. It was divided into three squadrons; the Van, wearing white ensigns, the Centre with red ensigns, and the Rear with blue ensigns. Each squadron had three flag-officers; an Admiral, Vice-Admiral and Rear-Admiral, each flying a flag of the colour of their squadron at the mainmast head, foremast head or mizzenmasthead respectively. They ranked in descending order of seniority in Red, White and Blue Squadrons, and the overall command was held by the Lord High Admiral in person, or an Admiral of the Fleet, who took the place of an Admiral of the Red Squadron. There were therefore nine flag officers in the Navy; the Admiral of the Fleet (if appointed) the most senior, followed by the Admiral of the White, and so on down to the Rear-Admiral of the Blue.

Though the operational organisation of the Navy rapidly became more complex, this scheme of flag ranks remained basically unchanged until 1864. From 1743 more than one flag officer of each rank on full pay existed, but they continued to rank with one another according to the seniority of their 'squadrons', and HM ships wore the red, white or blue ensigns depending on which 'squadron' their commander-in-chief belonged to. In 1805 the rank of Admiral of the Red was instituted, making ten flag ranks in all, and from 1862 there was sometimes more than one Admiral of the Fleet. In 1864 the notional 'squadrons' were abolished, the flag ranks reduced to four, and the white ensign adopted for all HM ships.

These flag ranks of the Royal Navy should not be confused with the titles of Vice-Admirals and Rear-Admirals of England and Scotland, and Vice-Admirals of the maritime counties and colonies; honorific titles descending from deputies of the medieval Lords Admiral.

Last among the flag officers' ranks is the Commodore, a Captain ordered to hoist a broad pendant whilst in command of a squadron. While wearing his broad pendant the Commodore exercised most of the authority of a Rear-Admiral, but it was until very recently a temporary rank conferring no permanent seniority, and not an essential step between Captain and Rear-Admiral. In the seventeenth century it provided flag officers for detached squadrons; in the eighteenth and later it served as a means of promoting to independent commands deserving Captains too junior to be made Rear-Admirals.

Two distinct ranks of Commodore in fact existed, formalised in 1805 by the titles of 1st and 2nd Class Commodore. The senior Commodore was a Captain appointed commander-in-chief of a station or a detached squadron. Within the limits of his station or his orders no flag officer could outrank him and he answered directly to the Admiralty. The Commodore 2nd Class, now extinct, was a senior Captain ordered by his Commander-in-Chief to hoist a broad pendant and command a division of the squadron. This often happened in the eighteenth century when a flag officer commanding a squadron large enough to be divided in action into the traditional three divisions found himself with only one junior flag officer; he would then order the most senior Captain to hoist a broad pendant and command the Rear division. Commodores 2nd Class received no extra pay and commanded their own ships; Commodores 1st Cass were paid as Rear-Admirals and allowed a flag captain. Both reverted to Captain's rank and seniority on hauling down their pendants, and, formally at least, derived no permanent advantage over other Captains from their temporary promotion.

Captains

The rank of Captain, or post-Captain, is the most senior below flag rank. In essence he is the commanding officer of a substantial warship, and until 1860 it was only by being appointed to command of such a ship, a 'post ship', that an officer could attain 'post rank'. HM ships from the 1st down to the 5th Rate (6th Rate from 1713) were 'post ships', and those below were not. The distinction between 'post ships' and Commanders' commands then corresponded exactly to that between rated ships and non-rated, and were nearly to that between 'ships' properly so called (square-rigged on three masts, as almost all large sea-going vessels were), and vessels rigged as brigs, schooners, cutters, ketches or whatever. The term post-Captain thus serves to distinguish the rank of Captain from the job of captain of the vessel (not a post-Captain unless of a post ship), or a petty-officer's rating like captain of the mast, or the polite form of address of masters of merchantment as 'Captain X'.

A Captain took his seniority from his first commission to command a named post ship, but each successive command required a fresh commission. Only from 1860 were officers commissioned in the Navy as such, receiving no new commission until promoted, and not necessarily deriving their post rank from appointment to command a post ship.

Before the twentieth century, a Captain's eligibility for flag rank depended largely on seniority, so that the date of 'taking post' was critical to an officer's career. In the eighteenth century Captains who survived to reach the top of the list were held to be entitled to flag rank, and propriety forbade passing them over in favour more junior officers. This restricted the field of choice for promotion to flag rank to a small number of Captains, many of them elderly and unsuitable, and barred the choice of abler and younger men. To avoid this problem, there was instituted in 1747 the rank of Read Admiral without distinction of Squadron. In effect this was a compulsory retirement scheme for senior Captains who received the title and half pay of a Rear Admiral as a reward for long service, on the distinct understanding that their sea careers were at an end. These officers were generally known as 'yellow admirals'. By this means it was possible for the Admiralty to reach as far down the Captains' list as it desired, selecting the suitable candidates for active flag rank, and retiring the others as yellow admirals. Apart from limited superannuation, it was not possible until 1827 to retire a Captain in that rank.

Occasional appointments were made of a Captain of the Fleet or First Captain, being a Rear-Admiral or senior post-Captain borne in the flagship of a large squadron in addition to the flag captain, to assist the Commander-in-Chief.

Commanders

In the seventeenth and eighteenth centuries the word 'commander' was equivalent to the modern 'commanding officer', the captain of the ship regardless of his rank. Post-Captains were commanders, but so were lieutenants commanding the smaller men of war, and also, in common parlance, the masters of privateers and even merchantmen. Until 1794 no rank of Commander can be said formally to have existed.

In practice, however, the Lieutenants who commanded men of war — 'lieutenants in command', or 'lieutenant commanders', as they were sometimes called — were in a different position from other Lieutenants. The commander of a sloop, albeit only a Lieutenant, had a much more responsible position than the Lieutenant of a sloop, his second in command. Like Captains, Lieutenants received commissions not for rank in the Navy as a whole, but for specific jobs in specified ships. Lieutenant-commanders were commissioned as Commander of the vessel, or rather, 'Master and Commander', since from 1674 they were expected to act as their own Masters,. and for some reason the title settled in that form rather than the more logical 'Commander and Master'. It remained thus even after non-post vessels were allowed Second Masters in 1746, and later when the larger sloops received Masters.

Formally speaking, a Master and Commander still ranked as a Lieutenant according to his original seniority, but in practice it was the senior Lieutenants who became Commanders; it was experience in command which best qualified an officer for post rank, and long before 1794 the Admiralty was treating Master and Commander as an intermediate rank between Lieutenant and Captain. It remained possible, however, to proceed directly from one to the other without ever being a Commander.

The modern rank of Commander was formally instituted 1794, from which date post-Captains were promoted solely from the Commanders' list. Like post rank, it was obtained only by being commissioned to command a named vessel of the appropriate size — a Commander's command, smaller than a post ship, but larger than the little vessels which were still commanded by Lieutenants. To these Lieutenants the old descriptions of Lieutenant-commander or Lieutenant in Command descended.

It was not until 1827 that the rank of Commander was in some measure disconnected from the Commander's command. In the year of the First Lieutenants of line of battleships were made Commanders. In fact it became, and remains, the custom to refer to the second in command, the executive officer, of a large warship as 'the Commander', while the officer in command, who would formerly have been called 'the commander', is now 'the Captain'.

The two senses of the word captain are nowadays fairly distinct: 'the captain of the ship' refers the job, and says nothing about rank; 'Captain X' is a post-Captain in rank, whatever his employment. It was not always so. In the eighteenth century all commanders, whatever their rank, were usually addressed as 'Captain X', and so were (and are) the Masters of merchant ships. An officer addressed as 'Captain' might be a Post-Captain, a Master and Commander, or even a Lieutenant in command. Until 1827, therefore all Commanders would normally have been addressed as 'captain', and the custom became so well established that throughout the nineteenth century Commanders were usually addressed as 'Captain', even though they were not of post rank, nor necessarily commanding a ship.

Lieutenants

The Lieutenant was, originally, the Captain's lieutenant in the literal sense, his deputy and understudy. By the late seventeenth century the number of Lieutenants had multiplied, and in the late eighteenth century 1st Rates bore up to nine lieutenants, and so down the scale to sloops with only one. Like the other commissioned officers, the Lieutenant received a new commission for each new appointment. Until the end of the eighteenth century a Lieutenant's commissioned specified not only his ship but also his position as 1st, (2nd, 3rd etc.) Lieutenant, so that a fresh commission was required if he moved up or down a place; until 1860 a fresh commission was issued for each new ship. Although numbered Lieutenant's commissions no longer exist, the term 'First Lieutenant' remains in use for the job of second in command of a small ship, or deputy to the Commander of a larger ship. It should be emphasised that 'First Lieutenant' is now a job, not a rank, and the officer holding it might rank as anything from Sub-Lieutenant to Commander depending on the size of ship.

The Lieutenant was the most junior of the ancient commissioned ranks, and his first commission marked the real beginning of a man's career as a quarter-deck officer with prospects of command. Lieutenants were reckoned as gentlemen whatever their actual social origins.

It was possible for an officer to pass many years of his career as a Lieutenant, and during the nineteenth century it became common to distinguish, for many purposes of rank, pay and pension, between lieutenants of more and less than eight years' seniority. The distinction was convenient, but the terminology was cumbersome, and in 1914 a new rank of Lieutenant-Commander was instituted for all Lieutenants of eight years' seniority and over. Henceforward all Lieutenants could in usual circumstances expect automatically to be promoted Lieutenant-Commander at eight years' seniority. This new rank received the title of the old Lieutenants in command, but it was, and is, a rank and not a job.

Mates and Sub-lieutenants

In the seventeenth and eighteenth centuries, any person in the Navy could in principle pass the Lieutenant's examination and receive a commission providing he satisfied certain conditions of age and service, but in practice most 'young gentleman', candidates for commissioned rank, passed through a small number of ratings, one of which was Master's Mate. The Master's Mate was a senior petty officer, one of the ill-defined group of petty and warrant officers known as 'inferior officers'. He was, as his name implied, an assistant to the Master, learning navigation from him, and often aspiring to a Master's Warrant. Commissioned officers also needed to be navigators, so many would-be Lieutenants served for a while as Master's Mates.

Master's Mates were more highly paid than any other rating, and were the only ratings allowed to command any sort of vessel. They could pass an examination qualifying them to command prizes and tenders, and to act as Second Masters of vessels too small to be allowed warranted Masters.

In its traditional form of rating a Master's Mate, colloquially just 'Mate', served as an avenue of promotion either to warrant or to commissioned rank. To the nineteenth century mind this untidy mingling of social classes was objectionable, and in 1824 a rating of Master's Assistant was established for would-be Masters, leaving the Mates unambiguously as would-be Lieutenants. In 1840 Mate was formally established as an officer's rank next below Lieutenant, and in 1860 it was renamed Sub-Lieutenant. It then became, and is now the most junior commissioned rank and the only route of promotion to Lieutenant.

The term 'sub-lieutenant' had been in occasionally currency since the eighteenth century to described inferior officers second in command of men of war so small that they were allowed only a single commissioned officer, the Lieutenant in command. These 'sub-lieutenants' stood to the Lieutenant-commander as the Lieutenant of a sloop did to the Commander. From 1802 to 1814 the phrase was officially used of the Midshipmen and Master's Mates, qualified as Lieutenants but not yet commissioned, who acted as second in command of gunboats, schooners and the like.

The term 'Mate' was revived in 1912 as part of a scheme to provide accelerated promotion to commissioned rank for promising young ratings. After special training they could become Mates, ranking with Sub-Lieutenants, and proceed to Lieutenant on more or less equal terms with their contemporaries who had entered as Naval Cadets. In 1931 the distinction was abolished and the promotees from the lower deck became sub-Lieutenants.

Midshipmen

Like Masters's Mates, Midshipmen were originally senior petty officers, some but not all of whom were 'young gentlemen' aspiring to become Lieutenant. It was necessary from 1677 for all candidates for commissioned rank to have served at least one year as a Midshipman, and from 1703 at least two years. Because of this regulation the proportion of Midshipmen who were 'young gentlemen' rose steadily, until by the later part of that century the word Midshipman was being used colloquially almost as a synonym for 'young gentlemen'. This was not literally correct, for there were many young gentlemen who were not Midshipmen, and some Midshipmen who were not gentlemen, but it marked a progression which was virtually complete by 1794. From this date all newly rated Midshipmen may be regarded as would-be commissioned officers. Unlike the Mate, however, the Midshipman has never attained the dignity of a commission.

The number of Midshipmen in a ship, like that of all ranks and ratings, was fixed by an establishment for each rate of ship, so that it was impossible to bear extra Midshipmen merely because there were extra young gentlemen desirous of qualifying for Lieutenant. This bore particularly hardly on those young gentlemen under Admiralty, and not captain's patronage, since the captain fixed all ratings, and naturally favoured his protégés over others'. To accommodate the Volunteers per Order (1676-1729) and College Volunteers (1729-1816) a rating of Midshipman Ordinary existed. This was a supernumerary Midshipman, paid only as an Able Seaman and taking the place of a seaman on the establishment, but able to count his time towards the qualifying service for Lieutenant. From 1816 College Volunteers were rated simply as Midshipmen, but they were still conventionally distinguished as 'Admiralty Midshipmen'. In 1833 the Admiralty Midshipman was renamed Extra Midshipman and once more allowed to rate as supernumerary, as the Midshipman Ordinary had done until 1816 — and for the same reason, to safeguard the prospects of young gentlemen seeking their qualifying service. Unlike before 1816, however, all young gentlemen, whether or not under Admiralty patronage, were entitled to be rated Extra Midshipman after four years' service. All Midshipmen were from 1842 known simply as Midshipmen, without distinction.

The Extra Midshipman should not be confused with the Midshipman Extraordinary of the seventeenth century, a rating established in 1676 to provide temporary sea-going berths for unemployed commissioned officers, who at that date were mostly not entitled to half-pay. This rating did not survive the general introduction of half-pay, though unemployed commissioned officers did sometimes go to sea in the eighteenth century as Volunteers.

Cadets

It has been explained that the great majority of 'young gentlemen' who entered the Navy in the hope of rising to commissioned rank began their service in ratings which were neither specifically intended for, nor entirely occupied by them. Many were rated Able or Ordinary Seamen before they advanced to Midshipman or Master's Mate, but the most common rate was Captain's Servant. A Captain was allowed four servants for every hundred men in his ship. Very few of these 'servants' were actual domestics; they were boys, growing up to a career either as seamen or as officers depending on their education, background and luck. Their relations with their Captain were to some extent those of an apprentice to his master, or of a follower to his patron.

There was, however, a small but distinct class of young gentlemen who entered the Navy under Admiralty patronage. They were established in 1676 as Volunteers per Order, commonly known as 'King's Letter Boys'. They were borne by Admiralty order and were supposed to take precedence over the Captain's protégés. In 1733 this system was modified by the opening of the Royal Naval Academy, (from 1806 College), at Portsmouth, to which the Admiralty nominees went as Scholars of the Academy for a training course of three years or less, before going to sea as Midshipmen Ordinary. The capacity of the Academy was forty Scholars often less in practice, and its products formed only a very small proportion of the young gentlemen of the Navy.

For various reasons the College was never a great success, although expanded in 1816, and 1837 it ceased to admit young gentlemen, though it continued in existence as an institution of professional training for commissioned officers.

Meanwhile the methods of entry of the large majority of young gentlemen who went to sea under a captain's patronage had been reformed. In 1794 the rating of Servant was abolished, and in its place three specific ratings were established; Boys 1st Class, called Volunteers (future officers), Boys 2nd Class (future seamen, aged 15-17) and Boys 3rd Class (future seamen, aged 13-15, also acting as domestics). Volunteer (after 1824 Volunteer 1st Class) was now the proper first rating for a would-be Lieutenant from which he proceeded to Midshipman. In 1838, the year after the RN College had ceased to accept young gentlemen, the rating of College Volunteer was abolished. In 1839 1st Class Volunteers were obliged to pass an examination for Midshipmen, and in 1843 they became Naval Cadets, a term which had been in currency for some years. It remained the case at this date, and to a steadily diminishing extent up to 1914, that some Cadets entered the Service under the patronage of Captains, or Admirals. Naval Cadet remained the first rating of the young gentleman aspiring to become a Lieutenant from 1843 until Navy finally ceased to recruit its future officers as children.

Masters

Masters were, and still are, the commanding officers of merchant ships, and the original relationship of Master to Captain, in the Middle Ages, was of the professional seaman commanding an individual ship to the military officer commanding the squadron or expedition. During the sixteenth century it became normal for captains to command individual ships in wartime. By the late seventeenth century commissioned officers were invariably trained as seamen, and the position of the Master became that of the specialist in navigation and pilotage. Like other warrant officers, Masters tended to come from a lower social class than the commissioned officers, but their pay, and in many respects their status, approximated to that of Lieutenants, and they had to be well educated to discharge their duties. Masters invariably stood watches and were qualified to command H.M. ships on non-combatant duties. They were professionally examined by Trinity House, requalifying for successively larger rates of ship. Masters were almost always recruited from Master's Mates. The Master of the flagship of a large squadron was known as the Master of the Fleet, and this title continued to be used occasionally until recent times for the senior navigating officer of a fleet flagship.

Masters were the earliest warrant officers to rise in social and professional standing. By 1808, when they were officially recognised as 'Warrant Officers of Commissioned Rank' they were generally accepted among the wardroom officers — which represented the social test of gentility. Later in the nineteenth century Masters attained full commissioned rank, and their titles were changed to assimilate them to other commissioned ranks. By then it had become obvious that there was no need for a specialised Navigating Branch when all commissioned officers were trained as navigators, and from 1872 there were no further entries to the branch. Many of the younger officers transferred to executive rank, and the last of the remainder retired in 1912. The progress of the branch is set out in Table 4, in which the vertical columns represent individual ranks, rising in seniority from left to right, and progressing in time from top to bottom, the tinted area marking the accession to commissioned rank (*see* Table 4).

Surgeons

Surgeons were warranted to ships by the Navy Board having qualified by examination at the Barber-Surgeons' (from 1745 Surgeons') Company. From 1796 to 1806 they were both examined and appointed by the Sick and Hurt Board, from 1806 to 1816 by the Transport Board, from 1817 to 1832 by the Victualling Board, and thereafter by the Admiralty. They were the only medical officers of individual ships, and almost the only ones for the whole Navy, but Physicians were appointed to the naval hospitals and to large squadrons, and apothecaries, entitled Dispensers (later Pharmacists) to naval hospitals and hospital ships. The Surgeon was assisted by one or more Surgeon's Mates, inferior officers warranted by the Navy Board from candidates who had served

Table 4 Masters & Navigating Officers

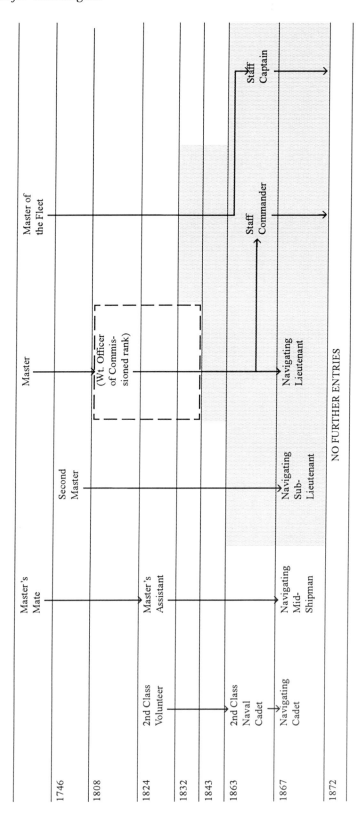

a regular apprenticeship to a surgeon or apothecary. The Surgeons were next after Masters in the rise to gentility and commissioned rank. In 1808 they became 'warrant officers of wardroom rank', for most practical purposes on a par with commissioned officers. Thereafter their progress may be simply charted (*see* Table 5).

Pursers

Pursers were warranted by the Admiralty and were not professionally examined, thought they had to provide financial sureties. Their duties were to oversee the supply and issue of victuals, slops (clothes) and other consumable ships' stores, partly as officials responsible for government stocks, partly as private contractors whose affairs were officially regulated. They might be assisted by a Steward and a Purser's Yeoman (or storekeeper), ratings who were in practice (though not in principle) selected by the Purser and usually paid their pay supplemented by him.

With Pursers it is convenient to consider Clerks, who were ratings employed to assist the Captain with the ships' books and paperwork. Their work was closely related to the Purser's, and a clerkship was a common training for a Purser's warrant. When the ranks came to be regulated and reformed in the nineteenth century Clerk was treated as a rank leading directly to Purser.

Flag officers had Secretaries to assist them with the administration of their squadrons. These Secretaries were often Pursers or former Pursers — sometimes they held the Purser's warrant for the flagship, with a deputy discharging these duties — but as Secretaries they were nominated by the Admiral. In the nineteenth century Secretary became an officer's rank (strictly ranks, varying with length of service and seniority of flag officer served) distinct from, and senior to Purser's rank, though always held by Pursers.

In the seventeenth and eighteenth centuries ships were paid only in port, as infrequent intervals, and no ship's officers were concerned with handling the money. In the nineteenth, however, it became customary to pay at first part, and later the whole of men's wages at regular intervals, for which purpose money had to be carried to sea, and the Purser was put in charge of it. This inspired a change of title to Paymaster and Purser, and later to Paymaster only, though the older term remains in colloquial usage. By this time Pursers, who like Masters and Surgeons had attained 'wardroom rank' in 1808, were advancing by stages to commissioned rank, and assimilating their titles to those of executive officers (*see* Table 6).

Table 5 Medical Officers

Year	Visiting Assistant, Assistant Surgeon & Assisting Dispenser	Surgeon's Mate	Surgeon	Surgeon (of a flagship or in charge of an establishment)	Physician	Inspector of Hospitals	[Higher grades]
1805	Hospital Mate and Dispenser					Inspector of Hospitals	
1815	(No further entries)	Assistant Surgeon				(abolished)	
1832							Physician of the Navy
1835							Physician-General of the Navy
1840					Deputy Inspector of Hospitals	Inspector of Hospitals	
1843							Inspector-General of Naval Hospitals and Fleets
1844	Pharmicist				Deputy Inspector of Hospitals and Fleets	Inspector or Hospitals and Fleets	
1855				Staff Surgeon			Medical Director-General
1859				Staff Surgeon 1st Class	Deputy Inspector General of Hospitals and Fleets	Inspector-General of Hospitals and Fleets	
1873		Surgeon	Staff Surgeon 2nd Class				
1875			Staff Surgeon	Fleet Surgeon			
1911					Deputy Surgeon-General	Surgeon-General	
1918		Surgeon Lieutenant	Surgeon Lieutenant-Commander	Surgeon-Commander	Surgeon-Captain	Surgeon-Rear-Admiral	MDG & Surgeon-Vice-Admiral

Table 6 Pursers & Paymasters

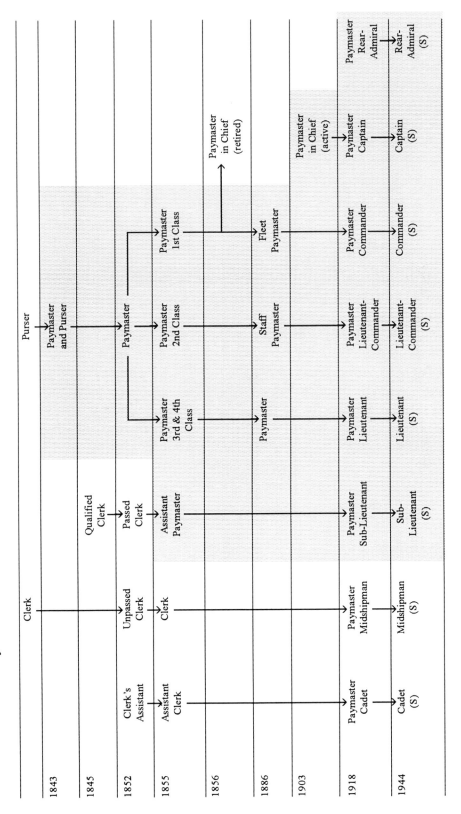

Engineers

The first engineers to enter the Navy were mechanics, often supplied by the firms which had built the ships' engines, and when the first Engineers' ranks were established in 1837 they included no commissioned ranks. The most senior Engineers became commissioned officers in 1847, and thereafter the branch passed through similar changes of title to the other civil commissioned ranks. It was, however, unique as a branch in that from 1847 to 1877 it was split between commissioned officers and those appointed by order, but treated as warrant officers. This means that the records of Chief Engineers and Inspectors of Machinery are often in different places from those of Engineers and Assistant Engineers, and different pension arrangements applied to those who reached commissioned rank, and those who did not.

In 1903 a new method of training executive officers, known as the Selborne Scheme, came into force, by which a common entry and training was split into executive and engineer branches only at Lieutenant's rank. Those who elected to become engineers were called Lieutenants (E), while the products of the former scheme of separate entry remained Engineer-Lieutenants. In 1925 common entry was abandoned, but the products of the revived engineers' entry scheme were ranked as officers (E), so that the older terms died out as their holders retired. In 1926 commissioned officers from warrant rank changed from Engineer to (E) titles.

The successive changes of Engineer officers' ranks and titles may be set out in a chart similar to those of other ranks (*see* Table 7).

Boatswains

The Boatswain's title was probably the most ancient of all officers', and in Anglo-Saxon times Boatswains actually commanded ships. By the seventeenth century, however, the Boatswain had sunk in social and professional standing. He was especially responsible for rigging and ground tackle, and kept the ship's stores of cordage, sails and associated gear. Boatswains were usually promoted from Boatswain's Mates. They were not eligible to command ships, but sometimes stood watches. Although like other warrant officers they kept accounts and made written reports, they tended to be less educated men than Masters, Surgeons and Pursers, and did not share their rise to commissioned rank. In the late nineteenth century limited opportunities of promotion to commissioned rank were made available, but in 1945 Boatswains remained warrant officers as they always had been. The warrant rank of Signal Boatswain was initially a specialisation, but from 1902 was treated as a separate rank.

Table 7 *Engineers*

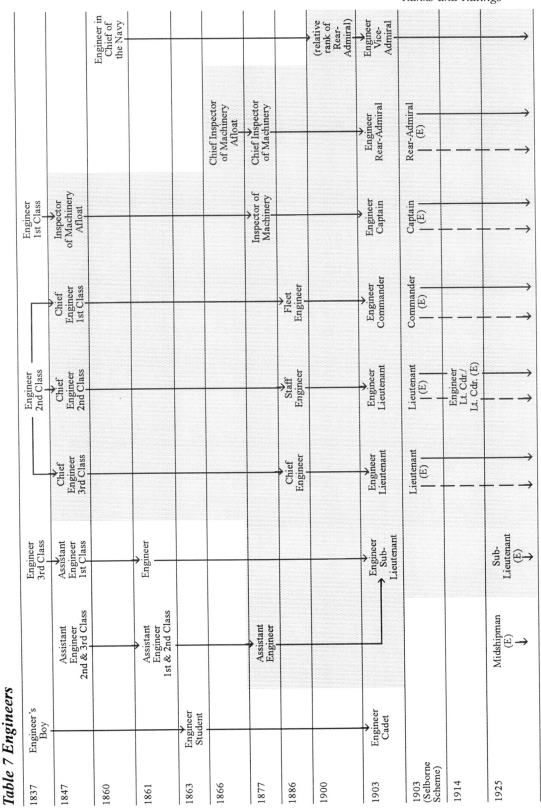

Gunners

The Gunner was a warrant officer who was particularly responsible for the ship's guns and ammunition, for which he accounted to the Ordnance Board. Gunners were assisted by, and usually recruited from Gunner's Mates, and their subordinates also included the Armourer, the Yeoman of the Powder Room and one Quarter Gunner, or seaman gunlayer, for every four great guns. Like Boatswains, Gunners remained warrant officers but from the late nineteenth century received limited opportunities of promotion to commissioned rank. From 1880 the lists of gunners included Gunners (T) or Torpedo Gunners, who specialised in torpedoes and mines, and were responsible for part of the ship's electrical equipment.

Carpenters

The Carpenter was a warrant officer responsible for the maintenance of the hull and masts of the ship. Carpenters were unusual in that many of them passed part of their careers as civilian employees of the Navy Board in the dockyards, and part as officers in the Navy. Although it was possible to serve an apprenticeship afloat as Carpenter's Crew and Carpenter's Mate, the majority qualified as shipwrights in the dockyards before going to sea, and some of the Master Shipwrights and their Assistants were former Carpenters who had returned to the yards.

Until 1918 the term Shipwright was not used for officers in the Navy, but in that year Carpenters, whose work had ceased to be entirely concerned with timber, were renamed Warrant Shipwrights. Like Boatswains and Gunners, they remained warrant officers in 1945.

Chaplains and Naval Instructors

Chaplains have always occupied an anomalous position. In the seventeenth and eighteenth centuries they were warrant officers, appointed by the Admiralty, and usually messed in the gunroom with the other warrant officers. In 1808 their pretentious to gentility were recognised by the grant of 'wardroom rank', and in 1812 they were established as pensionable officers. They remained warrant officers until 1843, when they first received commissions. It was then and remained for much of that century a matter of doubt how, or indeed if Chaplains ranked with other officers, and as they had no uniform, the question of marks of distinction did not arise. In the twentieth century it has come to be accepted that Chaplains are persons of wardroom status, appointed by the Admiralty and subject to naval discipline, but holding no particular rank. They may, but except in wartime usually do not, wear an officer's uniform without distinguishing marks.

With Chaplains it was convenient to consider Naval Instructors, who were listed with them in many service records. The Schoolmaster of the eighteenth century Navy was an inferior warrant officer, paid as a Midshipman, but of lower status. His duties were to instruct all young persons, whether future officers or not. In 1812 and again in 1816 the pay of the Schoolmaster was increased, in 1819 the qualifying examination was transferred from Trinity House to the RN College Portsmouth, and in 1822 the examination standard was raised. By this time some Chaplains were also acting as Schoolmasters, and in 1836 their status was equalised by the appointment of Schoolmasters as full warrant officers. In 1837 their title became Naval Instructor and Schoolmaster, in 1842 Naval Instructor, and in 1861 they received commissioned rank. From 1864 the ranks were divided by seniority. By this time many Chaplains were also acting as Naval Instructors, indeed this was the usual arrangement, and remained so until the Naval Instructor Branch was closed in 1903. The branch was revived in 1915, quite distinct from the Chaplain's Branch, and in 1918 Naval Instructors adopted executive ranks, from Instructor Lieutenant up to Instructor Captain.

The raising pay and status of the Naval Instructors (ex Schoolmasters) went with a concentration on teaching Cadets and Midshipmen, future officers. To take their place as teachers of boys and seamen a petty officer's rating of Seaman Schoolmaster was created in 1837. This was the first of the new rating branches to have the chance of advancement to warrant rank, in 1867, and subsequently to commissioned rank. These commissioned warrant officers of the Schoolmaster branch were quite distinct from the Instructor Officers who descended from the old Schoolmaster.

Cooks

Cooks were originally reckoned as warrant sea officers, but their status declined, and from 1704 when their warranting authority changed from Admiralty to Navy Board, they were regarded as inferior officers. For some purposes including pension, however, they continued to be treated on the same footing as warrant sea officers well into the nineteenth century. Cooks were usually recruited from disabled seamen, and were untrained.

In 1838 Cooks were defined as petty officers, but like other ratings they eventually acquired opportunities to advance to warrant and commissioned rank, so that from 1910 a small proportion of Cooks were able to reach and even pass the rank held by their predecessors in the sixteenth and seventeenth centuries.

Masters at Arms

The Master at Arms was an inferior officer appointed by Admiralty warrant, whose original duty was to instruct the ship's company in the use of small arms. He was assisted by a petty officer called the Corporal. The establishment of a permanent corps of Marines in 1755 tended to reduce the need for seamen to be trained in musketry, and emphasised a tendency for the Master-at-Arms to be employed as a species of ship's policeman. In the nineteenth century, like other inferior officers, he sank to the rating of a petty officer and his role in charge of the ship's police was formalised. Like other specialised ratings, Masters-at-Arms later received opportunities of advancement to warrant and commissioned rank.

Yard Officers

Until its abolition in 1832, the Navy Board was entirely responsible for the management of the dockyards, and the yard officers were civilian officials of that Board — 'Naval Officers' in the old sense. The senior appointments were however in the Admiralty's gift, and certain of them were usually reserved for former or half-pay sea officers, so records of these employments are mixed up with those of the Navy. These officers were the Commissioners, the heads of each yard, who were usually Captains on half-pay; the Masters Attendant who acted as harbourmasters and pilots, superintended yard craft and ships in reserve, and were usually former Masters; the Boatswains of the yard who were in charge of various labourers and were usually former Boatswains; and the Master Shipwrights, especially of overseas yards, who were sometimes former Carpenters. In addition there were some former warrant or inferior officers among other master craftsmen, and among the dockyard clerks. Each yard had a Surgeon and Chaplain who were normally recruited from the Navy, though they counted as Yard Officers.

After 1832 the yards continued to be run by a mixture of civilians and naval officers, but the latter were usually on full pay and appointed as part of their naval careers.

Coast Guard

The Coast Guard, which was under Admiralty control from 1857 to 1923, consisted of distinct organisations, several of which had, even before 1857, been largely officered by half-pay naval officers, and manned by former naval ratings. There are therefore many service records either of, or relating to Coast Guard Officers and ratings. (*See* Appendix III.)

Artificers

Until the late eighteenth century the Sailmaker was almost unique in the category of dockyard artificer who could be warranted as an inferior officer at sea. Caulkers, Ropemakers and Coopers were then added, but during the nineteenth century all reverted to being ratings.

Miscellaneous

Under this heading may be mentioned such of the 'new' warrant ranks not previously treated, certain quasi-officers or civilians in uniform like Naval Constructors and Canteen Managers, foreign officers serving in the Royal Navy, Nursing Sisters, Pilots, and other categories not otherwise covered.

Ratings

The number of rating which have been in use in the Navy is several thousand, which it is neither possible nor necessary to describe individually, since in the records ratings are generally to be found together, either for the Service as a whole, or for each individual ship. Until the introduction of Continuous Service in 1853 the principle source of information on ratings is the Musters and Pay Books (See Chapter IV).

CHAPTER THREE

Types of Service Record

The naval administration never evolved a standard method of keeping records of service, or a consistent terminology for referring to them. Methods of collecting and preserving information about individuals varied greatly at different periods and in different offices, and varied terms were used for the same or similar records. It is therefore impossible to describe the records in any clear and consistent way using the original descriptions, and for the purposes of this work the records have been classified into thirty-two standard types. Many of these were used only for officers, some only for ratings, and some for both. Throughout this book the same words are used for the same sorts of records, but the reader should be warned that this is by no means the case in the records themselves. The standard classifications are as follows:

1 Analyses

The Navy first felt a serious need to collect information about the age, former services and qualifications of its officers in the early nineteenth century, and especially after the peace of 1815, which left the service with about ten times as many officers as it could actually employ, and virtually no means of retiring them. When so few could be chosen for service, it was acutely important to select the right ones, and the information having been collected (see 23. *Surveys*), a variety of analyses were prepared of officers of particular ranks and branches, comparing ages, seniorities and numbers available and likely to be required. Many of these date from the 1840s when the difficulties of choice for promotion and employment were most acute. They differ greatly in form; some summarise the services of named individuals, while others give only overall figures.

2 Applications

It has always been customary to some extent, and was formerly much more common than it is now, for officers, and occasionally ratings, to apply for promotion or for particular appointments, or for their friends and patrons to apply for them.. In addition Admirals and Captains applied for those they wanted to serve under them. Records of these applications are probably more common among private than official papers, but many survive in the PRO, mostly in the form of entry books noting the applications, but including some original letters. The applications usually state the individual's former service or other claims to favour. There are some records of applications for nominations as Naval Cadets.

3 Appointments

Until 1860 officers were appointed to ships by individual *Commissions* or *Warrants* (q.v.), but there were certain temporary and shore duties to which officers were assigned only by Admiralty orders, not traceable in records of commissions and warrants. The records of these are here referred to as Appointments; they include acting captains of ships, and officers appointed to the Sea Fencibles, Cutters, Revenue Cruisers and Signal Stations. Ratings were appointed to these services in a similar fashion.

4 Black Books

A small collection of records was kept by the Admiralty and Navy Boards of the names of officers who had misconducted themselves in such a way that they were not to be employed again. They normally specify the nature of the offence and the name of the offender only.

5 Commissions

Commissions have always been the means by which commissioned officers take rank in the Navy, and until 1860 they were the only means of appointment to individual ships. Records of commissions kept by the Admiralty, usually in the form of entry books in chronological order, are for the seventeenth and eighteenth centuries the principle source of information on the successive employments of commissioned officers. Records of commissions also include fee books in which Admiralty or Navy Office clerks recorded the fees customarily paid on the issue of commission, or the fees still owing on commissions sent out to officers at the outports (i.e. away from London). There are also records of commissions issued by commanders-in-chief overseas, and some original commissions issued abroad and sent to the Admiralty for confirmation. The commission itself was a formal document conveying nothing material but the fact of the appointment and the name of the appointee.

6 Candidates for Promotion

The acute difficulty of selecting officers for promotion in the nineteenth century gave rise to another species of record, closely related to applications, in which the names and services of candidates for promotion were recorded and compared. Many of these records are in the form of notebooks compiled in the private offices of First Lords or First Naval Lords from information furnished by other departments, and there are also some original returns of this nature. Much of the information is simply abstracted from records of service which were, and often still are available elsewhere, but there is also some personal comment and assessment not recorded in formal records of service.

7 Certificates of Service

To quality for their commissions, warrants and pensions, officers and ratings had to prove their qualifying service, which they did by certificates issued by the Navy Pay Office containing an abstract of successive employments derived either from the Full and Half Pay Lists (for officers) or the Ships' Musters (for ratings). Before the introduction of service registers for officers and Continuous Service for ratings, both in the mid-nineteenth century, these certificates issued by the Navy Pay Office (after 1832 the Navy Pay section of the Account-General's Department) formed the only official evidence of the careers of officers and ratings. Departments which needed this information requested it from the Pay Office, and collections survive both of the original certificates as received, and of the Pay Office's entry books of the certificates as issued. It is in the nature of these documents that they record services only up to the date of issuing; those issued in connection with pension claims are the only ones which usually record an entire career. However recipient departments sometimes annotated their certificates with later information, and bound volumes of such are annotated certificates in fact form the earliest *Service Registers* (q.v.). The certificates of service give only the ranks or ratings of the subject, the ships served in and length of time in each..

8 Confidential Reports

From the mid-nineteenth century commanding officers were required to submit annual confidential reports on the character and abilities of their officers. These 'flimsies' hardly ever survive in their original form, but there are a few entry-books of returns compiled in the Admiralty. Most service registers contained printed columns in which the confidential reports are summarised under various headings.

9 Disposition Lists

At different dates various lists were kept by naval departments of the officers of a particular rank or branch with the posting or employment of each. They are not common, as *Service Registers* (q.v.) provided the same information in more detail, and the *Navy List* provides complete quarterly disposition lists.

10 Examinations

From the seventeenth century some officers were required to pass an examination or examinations to qualify for their commissions and warrants. In the nineteenth century the number and range of qualifying examinations increased greatly, and from this period survive the earliest results of examinations (as distinct from certificates of the fact of passing, for which *see* 18 *Passing Certificates*). The records are varied and fragmentary, but most give the marks obtained in various subjects, and some include candidates who failed.

11 Honours and Awards

This classification chiefly covers medal rolls which include campaign medals, various decorations for gallantry or good service, and record of honours and awards of all sorts. Some early entry-books appear to have been kept by the editors of the *Navy List* and include information about deaths.

12 Leave Books

These records are concerned either with ordinary leave given to officers on full pay to be absent from their ships, or with permission to officers on half pay to live or travel abroad. They consist chiefly of entry books in chronological order.

13 Marriage Certificates

A regulation of 1862 required married officers to submit marriage certificates as a condition of eligibility of their wives for widow's pensions. A small collection of those submitted survives, though the majority appears to have perished. The details of officers' marriages were however entered in service registers. Papers concerning widows' pensions and claims to Bounty often include marriage certificates.

14 Casualty Records

Registers and papers concerned with claims for and payments of the Bounty to the next-of-kin of officers and men killed in battle (*see* 16 *Pensions to Widows and Orphans*) form the earliest casualty records. They include many certificates of birth and marriage, and information about the addresses and circumstances of the beneficiaries.

Registers of claims to the back pay of seamen and marines dying in service, besides indexing the claims themselves (*see* 27 *Wills*) can be used as a source for the names of casualties and their next of kin. A small number of surviving nineteenth-century entry books noting the deaths of officers both serving and retired may have been kept by the editors of the *Navy List*, in which an Obituary List appeared. In addition there are registers and indexes of casualties from the mid-nineteenth century, mostly distinguishing deaths by enemy action from other causes, and some dealing with ratings or officers only.

15 Half Pay

Half Pay was a retainer for the services of unemployed officers, first paid in the 1660s to certain flag officers and Captains, and later extended to other officer at various dates, thus:

Admirals:	1668-ca.1689, 1697ff.
Commodores:	1675-ca.1689, 1697ff.
Flag Captains:	1668-ca.1688, 1697ff.
Captains of 1st Rates:	1674-ca.1688, 1697ff.
Other Captains:	1697ff.
Commanders:	1715ff.
Lieutenants:	1697ff.
Mates and Sub-Lieutenants:	1840ff.
Masters of 1st Rates:	1674-ca.1689, 1697ff.
Other Masters:	1697ff.
Surgeons:	1729ff.
Pursers:	1814ff.
Chaplains:	1817ff.
Engineers:	1856ff.

In the absence of any general schemes of retirement before the mid-nineteenth century half pay frequently operated as a species of superannuation, and no test of actual fitness to serve was until then applied. Thereafter half pay declined in importance, becoming simply means of filling short gaps in the careers of serving officers, and in 1938 it was abolished. Half pay records are mainly lists of names and the sums payable to them, but they sometimes include addresses and other information. In conjunction with Full Pay Registers they can be used, as they were in compiling certificates of service, to present an officer's full career.

16 Pensions to Widows and Orphans

From the seventeenth century to the nineteenth there were four principal bodies paying naval pensions of various types; the Admiralty (or rather the Navy Pay Office acting under Admiralty authority), the Chatham Chest, Greenwich Hospital, and the Charity for the payment of Pensions to the Widows of Sea Officers.

The Admiralty paid pensions chargeable on the Navy Estimates under the authority of Orders in Council in favour either of named individuals or of specified classes of officer. These included, from 1673, pensions to the widows of commissioned officers killed in action or as a consequence of service, which are referred to in Appendix I as Admiralty Pensions, though after 1830 this was only one of several pensions paid by the Admiralty. From 1809 the Admiralty also administered the Compassionate Fund (later the Compassionate List) voted by Parliament, which paid grants and pensions to the orphans or other dependants of officers killed in action. From 1830 warrant officers' widows were eligible for Admiralty Pensions, and from 1885 their dependants were eligible for the Compassionate List.

The Chatham Chest was a naval charitable foundation dating from 1590, supported by a charge of 6d. a month on the wages of every man in the Navy. It paid pensions to the widows of warrant officers, ratings and dockyard workers killed in action or on service. In 1803 it was transferred to the management of Greenwich Hospital and in 1814 extinguished as an independent fund, its pensions being combined with those of the Hospital.

Greenwhich Hospital was another charitable foundation, supported by 6d. a month deducted from the wages of both naval and merchant seamen, as well as by the wages of deserters, unclaimed prize money, the rents of estates forfeited in the 1715 rebellion and other income. In its original form Greenwich Hospital paid no widows' pensions as such, but it employed seamen's widows as nurses in its infirmary, and it provided a school for the children of officers and men, to which orphans had priority of admission. (*See* 29 *Schools Papers*).

After the closure of Greenwich Hospital as an institute accepting resident pensioners in 1869, it continued as a fund distributing various pensions, and running a school, now the Royal Hospital School, Holbrook, to which are admitted the sons of officers, seamen and fishermen of all services. It also offers education grants to the orphaned or needy children of naval officers.

The Charity for the payment of Pensions to the Widows of Sea Officers was established in 1732. Though administered by trustees, it was in fact more an official pension fund than a private charity. Its income derived from Parliamentary grants and a compulsory deduction of 3d. in the pound from officers' wages. It paid pensions to the poor widows of all sea officers regardless of how or when they had died, but not to those who were left comfortably off. In 1830 the entitlements to widows' pensions was removed from all warrant officers warranted from that date (unless killed in service), and was not restored until 1864. In 1836 the responsibility for officers' widows' pensions was assumed by the Admiralty, and the test of poverty abandoned. Engineers' widows received pensions from 1849.

The responsibility for paying all naval pensions was taken over by the Admiralty during the nineteenth century, leaving only Greenwich Hospital as an independent body paying various supplementary and special pensions. In general, however, the old distinctions between the types of payment made by the different funds remained, and for convenience in Appendix I the same terminology has been used throughout.

In addition to these pensions, a lump sum of one year's wages known as the Royal Bounty was paid to widows, dependant children or indigent mothers aged over 50 of officers, ratings and marines killed in action. (*See* 14 *Casualty Records*).

17 Other Pensions

Besides *Pensions to Widows and Orphans* and *Superannuation* (q.v.), various special pensions were payable in certain circumstances. From 1673 the Admiralty paid pensions for wounds to commissioned officers and Masters, later also Surgeons. These pensions were tenable in conjunction with full or half pay or superannuation. Similar pensions (for permanent disablement) or grants were paid to wounded warrant officers and ratings by the Chatham Chest, on production of a certificate commonly known as a 'smart ticket' (examples are in ADM 82/126-127). From 1866 warrant officers and Engineers were eligible for pensions for wounds, and from 1902 Midshipmen and Naval Cadets. A limited number of Greenwich Hospital Out-Pensions (for which *see* 20. Superannuation) were from 1814 given to Captains, Commanders and Lieutenants, while from 1871 some Greenwich Hospital Pensions (including pension paid from special funds like the Travers, Popeley and Canada Funds) were paid to deserving commissioned or warrant officers. In 1837 Good Service Pensions were created to replace the sinecure general ranks of Royal Marines, abolished in that year. Like them they were paid to deserving flag officers and Captains, and later to civil officers of equivalent rank. They could be held with full or half pay, but were forfeited on promotion.

18 Passing Certificates

From the 1660s 'young gentlemen', had pass an oral examination in seamanship to qualify for their first commissions, and professional qualifying examinations were later established for most warrant officers. In the nineteenth century qualifying examinations for all sorts became common among all junior officers and some specialist ratings. Passing certificates usually record only the fact of passing, sometimes with some comments. (For detailed results of written examinations *see* 10 *Examinations*).

19 Full Pay

The are records, normally in the form of ledgers, of payments to commissioned, and later warrant officers who were actively employed. They normally give only the officer's name and the exact dates of each employment, but they can be used, as they were for the *Certificates of Service* (q.v.) to compile a record of an officer's successive employments.

20 Superannuation

The concept of a retirement pension, paid automatically to all who had served for a given number of years or to a fixed age, as a reward for their former services or contributions, came late and slowly to the Navy. Until well into the nineteenth century no officers or ratings were entitled to superannuation, and the limited number of pensions available were regarded as a privilege to be granted to deserving candidates. In the absence for regular superannuation, half pay served a similar purpose for those who were entitled to it.

For the four pension-paying authorities (*see* 16 *Pensions to Widows and Orphans*), two paid superannuation or retired pay. The Admiralty, under the same procedure as applied to widows' pensions, paid individual retirement pensions to flag officers, some Captains, commissioners of dockyards, and various miscellaneous grantees such as foreign pilots. From 1672 a fixed number of the most senior warrant officers were entitled to superannuation, and this was in 1737 extended to the thirty senior Lieutenants, and in 1747 to 'Yellow Admirals'. All these pensions were paid on the same estimates as 'Admiralty' widows' pensions and pensions for wounds, with which they were generally listed.

The principle source of superannuation for unwounded ratings was Greenwich Hospital, which paid small Out-Pensions to deserving applicants who had served in the Navy or Marines, and admitted a fixed number to live as In-Pensioners of the Hospital. Both In- and Out-Pensions were available only on application, but there was no limit to the latter (except the Hospital's income) and the number of recipients was very large. Out-Pensions were a form of superannuation in that the claimants had to show former service in the Navy or Marines (twenty-one years' service from the age of twenty, after 1832), but there was no bar to them holding other employment, and the pensions were by themselves scarcely sufficient to live on. Many Out-Pensioners of the Hospital were still young men in full employment, and it was possible for both In- and Out-Pensioners to re-enter the Navy, when their pensions lapsed until their discharge. Warrant Officers were also eligible for Greenwich pensions, and from 1814 there was a small number of out-pensions for Captains, Commanders and Lieutenants. (*See* 17 *Other Pensions*).

At various dates from 1836 officers became eligible for superannuation, either automatically or upon application, on reaching a specified age and seniority. The first retirement pension for ratings was introduced in 1813. Those who had served at least 21 years were eligible, reduced to 14 years in 1825. In 1853 pensions of varying amounts were payable for service from ten to twenty years from age 18. By 1853 Continuous Service for ratings was introduced, with the incentive of a pension for all who served twenty years. The majority of ratings thereafter entered as boys, signed their first engagement at eighteen, and therefore retired at about 38, or 43 for those who signed on for a 'fifth five'. This left a man much of his working life, and naval pensioners often were (and are) still working. Indeed the Navy employed pensioners in many duties in dockyards and naval establishments. Few records of pensions to ratings survive, but from the Continuous Service engagements (*see* 30 *Entries*) and *Service Registers* (*see* 21) it is possible to tell who received pensions.

21 Service Registers

The practice of keeping all information about an individual officers' career in a single record seems first to have been undertaken by Pepys, and not again attempted until the 1840s. The earliest modern officers' service registers consist of annotated *Certificates of Service* (q.v.) bound into volumes. They always include the officer's full name, successive ranks and appointments. Later service registers, kept in volumes printed especially for the purpose, also include much other information, such as assessments of character and ability, notations of praise or blame for particular incidents, dates of birth, marriage and death, names of parents and wives (but almost never of children), and details of pay and pension.

At least in the nineteenth century, it was usual for officers' service registers to be kept by many departments, and an individual's career may sometimes be entered in three or four more-or-less identical registers kept in different offices. This helps to compensate for the numerous gaps in the surviving series.

The dating of service registers present particular problems, for there were several methods of compiling them. Many of the earliest registers were begun in a particular year, showing all the officers of a particular branch then in service, or even then alive. Such a volume would probably be kept up to date so long as any of these officers remained in service, or alive. As space allowed, this or a successor volume would be used to enter the new officers joining the branch, and their subsequent services to the end of their careers. The most typical pattern was for each volume to contain the new entries for perhaps five or ten years, continued to the end of each officer's career or life, however short or long. Other departments kept service registers covering a fixed calendar period, ignoring the earlier or later services of those entered, so that only a single volume would be in use at any one time. Others again kept different registers for each rank, so that an officer's successive promotions involved transfers from one volume to another. Many series combined two or more of these methods, or changed from one to another. This makes it very unhelpful to give only outside dates. A register compiled in 1860, for example, and continued with new entries to 1865, might well cover officers whose earliest services dated from the eighteenth century, and others alive well into the twentieth. To date it '1790-1940' would be more accurate than useful when the volume was actively being compiled for only five years. In Appendix I therefore the words 'compiled', 'entries', 'service', 'promotions', and 'seniority' have been used, eg:

1846 (compiled)	(complete careers of those in service in that year)
1846-1848 (compiled + entries)	(complete careers of those in service in 1846, and of entries 1846-1848)
1848-1855 (entries)	(complete service of those entering in these years)
1870-1875 (promotions)	(careers from promotion only of officers promoted in these years)
1880-1885 (service)	(service between these dates only)
1780-1840 (seniority)	(service of officers of seniority within these dates; retrospective compilations, differing from 'entries' or 'promotions' by omitting those dead or retired)

The earliest service registers for ratings cover men entering the Service from 1873. They consist of loose forms bound up into volumes, and give similar, but rather less information than officers' Service Registers.

22 Succession Books

These were a type of officers' service record arranged not by the name of the individual but by names of ships. In the usual form a page was opened for each ship and the successive appointees to each officer's position in that ship listed. A succession book allowed its compilers to tell at a glance which officers were then serving, or had previously served, in a particular ship. Many of these books cover officers of a single branch only. Usually they have indexes to the names both of ships and officers, so an individual's career afloat can be followed from ship to ship. Succession books were for ratings were kept by the Coast Guard.

23 Surveys

At the peace of 1815 the Navy shrank in a few years from a strength of 145,000 to only 19,000. No means of retiring any officers existed except for Yellow Admirals and the small number of Lieutenants and warrant officers entitled to superannuation, so that the Navy found itself with approximately ten times as many officers as it required. When so few could be employed, it was important to choose the best men, and the Admiralty found it had very little information about its officers, and even less that was easily accessible. In particular, it had no idea of their ages and experience. It therefore turned to the only obvious source of information, the officers themselves. At various dates between 1817 and 1851 circular letters were sent to commissioned and warrant officers requesting them to furnish their dates of birth or details of their services. These returns were then bound up and used for reference in the Admiralty. Many officers never received or neglected to return their forms, many returns have been lost, and of those that survive not all are indexed. The memory, and indeed the veracity of officers recounting their own services are not always to be depended on. Nevertheless, these surveys are the most convenient and complete records of officers' services available before the general adoption of *Service Registers* (q.v.).

24 Seniority Lists

Lists of officers arranged in seniority, that is the chronological order of their commissions or warrants, were compiled from the seventeenth century, and are printed in the *Navy Lists*.

25 Unfit for Service

Registers were kept, and in a few cases have survived, of officers medically unfit for active employment.

26 Warrants

Records of warrants issued, like those of *Commissions* (q.v.) were maintained by the Admiralty and Navy Board, and returned by commanders in chief overseas. There are also some books recording fees paid or to be paid to the clerks who issued the warrants. The records give simply the name and ship of the recipient, and the date of issue of the warrant.

27 Wills

Copies or original wills made by officers and ratings are attached to many applications made after their deaths for their back pay. Registers of these claims and wills, in addition to their intended function can be used as *Casualty Records* (q.v.) and as sources for the names and relationships of next of kin.

28 Addresses

The Admiralty kept records of the addresses of its officers from the eighteenth century, but only one or two nineteenth-century address books survive. Addresses are often entered in the records; either the addresses of officers on full or half pay, the addresses of officers' or ratings' parents at time of entry, or the addresses of officers' next of kin at time of death.

29 Schools Papers

This class consists entirely of papers bearing on applications for admission to the schools administered by Greenwich Hospital. These were largely reserved for the children of officers and ratings of the Navy, and priority was given to those fathers had died or suffered in the Service. These papers therefore give information, often in detail, about the services of the applicants' fathers.

The original Greenwich Hospital School was founded some time about 1716. It admitted the sons of officers, ratings and marines, though commissioned officers' sons became uncommon as the century progressed. In 1805 it was joined by the Royal Navy Asylum, a private charitable foundation established in 1798 (under the name of the British National Endeavour) to educate naval orphans. The Asylum admitted boys and girls at ages between five and eleven, and the boys might (but did not necessarily) proceed to the Hospital School at thirteen. In 1821 the two schools were united in a single organisation, and in 1825 named the Upper and Lower Schools. From 1828 to 1861 a special school of commissioned (and from 1850 warrant) officers' sons was maintained, and no commissioned officers' children were admitted to the Lower School. In 1861 the schools were renamed the Nautical and Lower Divisions. From 1861 to 1949 no commissioned officers' sons were admitted to the school. In addition to the girls' class of the Lower School, abolished in 1841, there existed a small class for the infant children of Greenwich Hospital In-Pensioners and staff.

30 Entries

A variety of lists and papers were compiled, almost all of ratings, recording the date and circumstances of their entry into service. The earliest records of Continuous Service are of this type.

31 Discharges

The counterpart of *Entries*, and like these largely confined to ratings.

32 Musters

This includes a miscellaneous collection of nominal lists of ratings. For Ships' Musters *see* Chapter Four.

CHAPTER FOUR

Musters and Pay Books

Introduction

The keeping of musters — that is, lists of the ship's company — must have been necessary from the earliest time when warships were taken into the service of the Crown, and in fact musters survive in E 101 (Exchequer Accounts Various) and C 47 (Chancery Miscellanea) from a variety of mediaeval ships. Some musters of 1626 survive in SP 16/22-23. The keeping and preservation of musters was greatly improved by the initiative of Samuel Pepys, but most of the musters of this period appear to have been destroyed when the hulk *Eagle* was burnt at Chatham in 1685, and only a few survive from before this date.

Though the musters became progressively more complex, they adhered throughout their history to a basic pattern, already present in the musters of the 1670s, and still clearly to be discerned in the Ship's Ledgers of two centuries later. This present chapter takes as standard the musters in ADM 36 of the latter part of the eighteenth century, and provides a detailed description of them following by notes on the variations from that form shown by different classes. In general the nineteenth-century musters, though more complex, contain such complete and detailed instructions to the compiler that it is needless to explain them in great detail.

Purpose

In order to understand the musters, it is essential to understand their purpose, which was twofold. First they recorded the actual service of every person belonging to the ship or otherwise on board, in order to determine his wages. Next the books record his consumption of both victuals and articles chargeable to his wages, for the purpose of the Purser's accounts. The former aspect was the responsibility of the Captain and the latter of the Purser, and both these officers, together with the Master and Boatswain, signed each list within the musters. The passing of the Captain's and the Purser's accounts depended on the accuracy and completeness of the ship's books and errors or omissions could be, and often were, charged against their pay, so both officers had a strong incentive to keep the books as well as possible.

Preparation and Types of Muster

Both Captain and Purser (in practice often the Captain's Clerk and the Purser's Steward) kept a variety of rough musters for practical use. With two exceptions (noted below) these rough books were not preserved, but from them were written up in fair copy musters for return to the Clerk of the Cheque (the senior financial officer) of the dockyard which was the ship's home port. He forwarded them to the Navy Office, where they were 'set off' on the Pay Books in order to pay the ship. The musters are of two types: Monthly Musters, and General Musters or Open Lists, which in principle covered periods of two and twelve months respectively, though in practice there was much variation. Both types were returned and preserved, and are commonly bound together, so that each ship should be represented by six Monthly Musters and one Open List *per annum.* The Open List records each man's presence or absence for pay and victuals throughout the year, but omits the charges against his wages entered in the Monthly books.

Complement, Wages & Victuals

Each muster begins with a statement of a ship's name, or in the case of other vessels, name and type, and her complement as authorised by an order from the Navy Board. This was the maximum number of officers and men which she was permitted to bear on her books; any others had to be borne as supernumeraries and authorised by an order from a commander-in-chief or senior officer. There follows an exact statement of the periods from her original commissioning until the date of the muster that the ship had been in wages and victuals. In fact the commissioning date — the day, that is, on which the first captain arrived on board, and read his commission — was for administrative purposes an irrelevance in the eighteenth century. The ship was an administrative unit from the day, often months earlier, when the first officer arrived on board and hoisted the pendant, and from that day the musters commence. At first, however, the ship remaining in or off the dockyard was under the administrative control of the Clerk of the Cheque, who held the weekly musters, paid the men, and victualled them under 'petty warrants' signed by himself and the commanding officer and directed to the Agent Victualler. Only when the ship was ready to put to sea did she cease to be 'under the cheque' and enter on 'sea victualling', in the full control of her own officers. In the seventeenth century a similar distinction was recorded between 'rigging wages' and 'sea wages'. Whenever the ship returned to a dockyard port for any length of time she would again come 'under the cheque'. all the dates of beginning and ending sea and petty warrant (or 'extra petty warrant') victualling are recorded at the head of the muster. So are the dates of any period at sea on short allowance of victuals, for which the crew were entitled to 'short allowance money' in compensation.

Muster Table

Beneath the introductory note on the first page of each muster is a Muster Table, which records when, where and by whom each weekly muster had been held, and sets against each a 'muster letter' to be used for distinguishing it in the muster lists following. The Table also includes a tabular summary of the numbers recorded at each muster, divided into 'Ship's Company', 'Marines part of Complement', 'Supernumeraries for Wages and Victuals', and Supernumeraries for Victuals only'. The sum of the first two should be not more than the complement. Within each of the four sections are distinguished the numbers borne, mustered, 'chequed' and sick. Those borne were all those entered as belonging to that ship and paid in her, regardless of whether present or not. Those mustered were actually present at the weekly muster. Those chequed were noted as absent with leave for any reason except sickness, by a 'cheque' or tick against their names in the muster. Those missing without leave were likewise marked with a 'prick' or dot, and included on this total. Those sick were chequed absent ashore or elsewhere on account of sickness, but not actually discharged onto the books of a hospital or hospital ship. The first figure (numbers borne) should be the sum of the last three.

To understand these distinctions it is important to bear in mind that a man could be borne for wages in one ship and victuals in another. For obvious reasons he had to be victualled where he actually was, but he could be part of the complement of some other ship from which he had been lent or otherwise detached, by accident or design. He would then be borne for wages on his own ship, chequed absent, and as a supernumerary for victuals only in the ship on board which he actually was. Moreover many people might be on board and borne for victuals only, who did not actually belong to the Navy at all and were not being paid by it. Such were soldiers, passengers, prisoners of war, customs officers and shipwrecked mariners. Other supernumeraries for victuals only were pilots extra, admirals and their retinues, and men newly recruited by a tender and not yet entered on the books of any ship. Tenders were small vessels, not administratively independent, which kept their own musters for victuals only and bore their companies for wages on the books of a large ship. Prisoners of war and other passengers not engaged in the work of the ship were usually borne for victuals at two-thirds allowance only.

Muster Lists

Following the Muster Table, the muster contains a series of lists, each separately numbered and signed by the four 'signing officers', for each of the four main types of personnel on board, and in the case of supernumeraries for victuals only, for each separate group or category. At the end of the muster is a list of those 'run' (i.e. deserted) during its period, and a declaration from the Captain that they 'deserve no relief' (from the forfeiture of wages and prize money and the penalties prescribed by the Articles of War). This is accompanied by a list of those slain in action (if any), and a declaration that the Articles of War and the abstracts of the Act of Parliament relating to seamen's wages had been read monthly to the ship's company as the regulations prescribed and were posted up in some public place on board.

The lists are arranged in a series of columns, printed vertically across an opening, or in the case of the Monthly Musters before the mid-1750s vertically down each page turned sideways. The number of columns increased gradually during the century, but even before the addition of some of the new columns the information they were intended to show was often being entered in the margins.

Muster Column Headings

The muster columns as they were in the eighteenth century are as follows, reading from left to right:

No.
Each man had a unique number on his list, not duplicated or re-used by any other man during the commission (but see below, 'Split Books').

Entry & Year
This is the date and year on which the man was first borne on the ship's books, and from which he was paid whether or not actually then on board. In the case of sea officers it is the date of their commissions, warrants or orders; in the case of new recruits the date of their impressment or (if volunteers) of their accepting bounty. Blanks are generally to be read as 'ditto'.

Appearance
This is the date of the man's actual arrival on board, from which he was victualled as well as paid. It might or might not coincide with his entry, but could in no circumstances precede it. Blanks are 'ditto', either from the next date above, or from the entry date, whichever be the later.

Whence & Whether Prest or Not
This is a difficult column to interpret. There are three main and several minor categories of men distinguished, besides officers. Pressed men and volunteers are self-explanatory terms, and it was usual to add either the place on shore, or the merchantman at sea, from which they had been recruited, and if applicable the tender which had brought them on board. A 'rendezvous' was a recruiting post established by a party from the ship or by an officer sent by the Admiralty on the Impress (i.e. recruiting) Service. They were usually in inns in London or the larger seaports. Typical entries might therefore read: 'London rendezvous per *Love & Unity* tender pressed', or '*Harcourt*

Indiaman volunteer' — all heavily abbreviated. Blanks are often, but not always, to be interpreted as 'ditto', ignoring the interpolation of officers. Sea officers (noted as 'per commission', 'per warrant' or 'per order') and servants may be assumed always to be volunteers, and marines usually so. Men turned over from other ships, though they must have originally have been mostly pressed or volunteers, are treated as a distinct category. It is thus usually possible to distinguish a man from a town (noted as pressed or volunteer) from a man turned-over from a ship of the same name. An exception to this rule is men from the guard-ships which were in effect floating barracks supplying ships with draughts of newly raised men, who are distinguished as pressed or volunteers.

Besides these three main categories of men entering there are others which may be met with. Men 'in lieu' or 'substitutes' were seamen who had been persuaded (i.e. bribed) to volunteer by someone who had been discharged on condition of finding one or more substitutes. Other recruits were returned prisoners of war exchanged by cartel, enemy prisoners volunteering to serve, debtors discharged from prison under the provisions of the 1758 Navy Act,[1] and vagrants sent in by parish officers (though the last were seldom accepted into the Service). It was very common for men formerly discharged, for instance into hospital, to be re-entered, and there were frequent transfers between the ships' company and the supernumeraries, all of which are noted simply by the appropriate numbers.

If the ship commissioned from the Ordinary (i.e. the reserve) she would have already on board the five 'standing officers', the Boatswain, Carpenter, Purser, Cook and Gunner, (with their servants), who were permanently attached to the ship for her maintenance. While she was out of commission they were borne and paid on the Ordinary books of the yard (ADM 42), from which they are shown as turned-over on the commissioning of the ship. In theory, at least, these officers were already on board, and the turn-over a purely administrative change.

Age
This column, added in 1764, records the man's age at entry into the ship (not at the date of the muster). The ages of sea officers, servants, marines and supernumeraries for victuals only are usually omitted. Many officers altered this heading of the Marine List to state 'No. of Company'.

Place & Country of Birth
This column also was added in 1764, though not all officers were conscientious about filling it in for some years afterwards.

---

[1] 31° Geo: II c.10

No. & Letter of Ticket

Men discharged before the ship was paid off received a 'ticket' for their wages, encashable on board the day the ship paid off, and thereafter at periodic 'recalls' in the yard or at the Navy Pay Office in London. The counterfoils of the tickets were returned by the ship with the musters, and their identification letters and numbers entered therein as a security against fraud.

Men's Names

Persons of the same name are distinguished in the lists by '1st', '2nd' &c. The spelling of non-English names is often approximate at best. 'Widows' men 'were fictitious men, two in every hundred of the complement, borne at able seamen's wages which were assigned to the fund for paying officers' widows' pensions.

Qualities

In this column is entered the rank or rating of each man, with any changes during the period of the muster. The abbreviations are generally self-explanatory, but a few general points should be noted. All officers were allowed 'servants' in proportion to their rank, and the size of the ship. With a few exceptions, mainly among admirals' retinues, these were not domestics but boys, in effect apprenticed to their masters. There was no rating of 'boy' until 1794. Among the Captain's Servants will usually be found 'young gentlemen', sometimes his own sons, who were on their way to becoming quarter-deck officers. With one exception there was no rank or rate proper to the young would-be commissioned officers; they were borne in such rates as Servants, Able Seamen, Midshipmen or Masters Mate, and no formal distinction was made between them and the seamen and petty officers in the same rates. In practice it is often possible with an experienced eye to pick out 'young gentlemen' but only the rate of Midshipman Ordinary was effectively reserved for them. The great majority of would-be commissioned officers never served in this rate, and none did so for very long.

The 'quality' of supernumeraries and passengers of all sorts is not always stated, but among those which are may be found more or less accurate renderings of the ranks in various foreign services, besides such entries as 'baby', 'Indian squaw', and 'government serf' (a Russian prisoner).

D, DD or R

The letters stand for 'Discharged', 'Discharged Dead' and 'Run' (i.e. deserted). In addition there is Ds, 'Discharged to Sick Quarters', and occasionally DUS. 'Discharged unserviceable'. Dq and the more common Dsq represent the addition to D and Ds of a 'query', which acted as a stop to the payment of wages until removed by subsequent information. This process is more fully described under Pay Books, below.

Time of Discharge & Year
A discharge for whatever reason was an absolute one, so the date represents the end of a man's service. Men could be, of course, and often were re-entered later, for instance returning cured from hospital.

Whither or for What Reason
The common reasons for D include 'Request' (in wartime usually only by officers), 'Preferment' (promotion into another ship, sometimes specified), 'Superseded' (officers replaced for any reason), 'Unserviceable' (generally with the date of the admiral's order, and sometimes with mention of the medical survey), and 'With his Master' (servants). The most common of all is simply the name of another ship to which the man had been turned over. Unspecified discharges are in wartime always accompanied by a note of the admiral's or Admiralty order authorising them, often in the form 'pLO' (per Lords' Order) and the date.

DD is usually accompanied by a note of the circumstances; 'At Sea', 'Slain in Battle'. 'Fell from aloft'. Deaths may be assumed to be from illness unless otherwise indicated.

Men R are always noted as having run 'from the ship', 'from the boat', 'from leave', 'from lent' or whatever, and where.

Discharges to Sick Quarters always specify the hospital or hospital ship. The abbreviation 'HH' sometimes met in this context stands for Haslar hospital, and 'HS' for Hospital Ship.

> This is the last of the columns common to both Monthly and General Musters. The following columns recording deductions from wages appear only in the Monthly Musters.

Straggling
In wartime rewards were offered for the apprehension of 'stragglers' (deserters or men improperly absent from their duty). These rewards were chargeable to the offender's wages.

Neglect
The value of stores or gear lost or damaged by negligence might be deducted from wages.

Slop Clothes

Pursers were obliged to carry stocks, fixed according to the rate of the ship, of slops, that is clothes, which were sold to individual men. Until 1758 slops were supplied to pursers by one or more contractors whose names are printed at the head of sub-columns of the muster. In that year the Navy Board took over the supply of all slops.

Venereals

Men who had contracted venereal diseases were charged a sum of 15s, representing the cost of the medicines supposed to cure them, the sum being payable to the Surgeon. This was intended to deter them from putting themselves at risk of getting such diseases, but actually only deterred them from reporting sick.

Trusses

Ruptures were a common injury sustained by men handing sails aloft, and the Surgeon carried a supply of trusses for issue to the sufferers, at their expense.

Cloathes in Sick Quarters

For the prevention of infection (and also desertion) men received into hospital were stripped of their clothes and put into a sort of shift or nightshirt. The cost of this was charged to the men as for slops, but the financial arrangement was different, the hospital clothing being a government rather than a purser's issue.

Dead Men's Cloaths

It was the custom to sell the clothes and effects of a dead man 'by the mast' (i.e. at a public auction) for the benefit of the dead man's widow or next of kin. This was a disguised form of charitable collection, since greatly inflated prices were paid for common articles. The successful bidders had the prices charged against their wages, and the dead man received them credited to his.

Beds

Beds (hammocks, mattresses and blankets) were among the purser's stocks for sale to the men.

Tobacco

An important item, supplied by the purser on his own account for sale to the men.

Wages Remitted from Abroad

The 1758 Navy Act allowed men serving in ships abroad to remit wages to relatives on the same terms (i.e. yearly six months in arrears) as those in home waters were to be paid. In this column were entered the appropriate deductions.

Date of Parties Order for Allotting Monthly Pay

The 1795 Navy Act[1] established an improved mechanism for 'allotting' a proportion of pay to a named relative, which could be claimed at monthly intervals even if the ship had not been paid. Men desiring to allot their pay had to sign an order specifying where, to whom, and of course from what date their pay was to be allotted.

Two Months Advance

Two months' wages in advance were payable to volunteers on joining their ships, under the provisions of the 1758 Navy Act.

Necessaries Supplied Marines on Shore

Special financial arrangements applied to marines serving ashore but borne on a ship's books, who were issued with slops, mess traps etc.

To whom Tickets Delivered

The pay ticket of a man discharged from the ship would usually be given to him ('party'), or if not made out until after he had gone, sent to his new captain for him. Servants' tickets were given to their masters (who received their wages), dead and run men's tickets went to the Navy Pay Office, while others were given to agents, attorneys and relatives.

Muster Columns

A series of narrow columns, four to a month with spaces at the head to enter the months and the date of each muster; in an Open List there are twelve months' muster columns occupying the whole right-hand page, in a Monthly Muster only two months' muster columns. In the columns is entered the muster letter (derived from the Muster table) for every man present at each muster, and a cheque, prick or other note for each man absent but not discharged, with a note of the reason for his absence. Men chequed were most commonly on leave (abbreviated as 'Lv'), Lent ('Lt'—easily confused with 'Lv') or on service in a prize or tender. Men were lent either to another man of war, or to a merchantman in lieu of men pressed out of her. Men sent sick on shore (or to a hospital ship) as noted as 'Ss' (usually written as a single ligature). After 1756 all men away sick for more than a week were discharged with a ticket, to be re-entered later if they recovered and returned. Men absent without leave, but not yet run were pricked, and against their names of all men discharged for any reason a line is ruled through the columns. The exact dates of each man's leaving and returning is in all cases noted for the purser's victualling account.

Split Books

In the seventeenth century, the great majority of men of war commissioned only for a season, and paid off in the autumn. Their cruises were no longer than a

---

[1] 35° Geo: III c.28

merchantman's voyage, and there was little difficulty or inconvenience in leaving all payments until the ship paid off (assuming the money was then available). In the course of the eighteenth century, however, it became normal for fleets to keep the sea at all seasons, and individual ships to remain in commission for years at a time. This imposed great hardship on the men, especially on the minority who were married, and two Navy Acts in 1728[1] and 1758, attempted to enforce regular payments in the course of a commission. The earlier act became largely ineffective, but the 1758 Navy Act, sometimes called Grenville's Act, had a real impact. It required that ships in home waters should be paid, and men in ships abroad should have their opportunity to remit pay to their relatives, at least once a year, the pay to be not more than six months in arrears. In practice it was seldom less, and ships were not paid as frequently as every twelve months, but they were usually paid several times in the course of a commission.

When a ship was paid her musters were 'split' at the date to which she had been paid (*not* the date on which the payment had taken place) and new books were started, omitting all men discharged before the pay date, and re-entering the remainder from that date, entering under 'Whence' some phrase such as 'Former Books'. Most split musters continue the old numbers, which then represent a broken series, but a few improperly re-number the lists, with or without a crib from old numbers to new. In split books, the date of 'entry' represents simply the commencement of a new pay period, and it is necessary to look back into earlier musters to determine the actual date of entry. The period between the date to which, and date on which the ship was paid is commonly represented both by a rough muster in the old series, and a fair copy in the new. These rough musters usually contain only the muster letters and cheques without financial information. Similar rough musters are often included from periods under cheque, when they presumably represent the Clerk of the Cheque's working copies.

Description Books

Captains were required to keep books containing a physical description of every man on board, but they were not supposed to return them, and they are almost never preserved. Descriptions of deserters, taken from these books and sometimes written on pages torn from them, were to be sent to the Admiralty, and are sometimes to be found annexed to a Run List or enclosed with a letter in ADM 1.

Muster Alphabets

Only very rarely does an eighteenth-century muster contain an 'alphabet' (an index of surnames in alphabetical order of initial letter only), but it is worth noting that the

---

[1] 1° Geo: II St.2 c.14

corresponding Pay Books (ADM 31-35) often contain alphabets from about 1765, and may thus be used as a means of reference (if not as a substitute) for the musters.

Muster Classes

ADM 39

This miscellaneous collection of unbound musters contains the oldest in the PRO, but differs from those in ADM 36 &37 only in its provenance. These musters are copies kept by the Clerk of the Cheque at Deptford of the musters of ships under his cheque, the fair copies of which, returned to the Navy Office, are mostly in ADM 36. The class, which should properly be considered among yard records, also includes musters of the Deptford yachts, hoys, hulks, tenders, hospital ships and yard craft.

ADM 36 & 37

The nature of the documents of these classes have been noted in detail. There is no distinction between the musters in ADM 36 and those in the earlier part of ADM 37, but there is a break within ADM 37, occurring between 1828 and 1836 (the exact date varies from ship to ship). The musters then assume a new and slightly more elaborate form, which is largely explained in the books themselves. The list distinguishes, more or less inaccurately, between various types of muster thus:

'C'   A Complete Book, equivalent to the former Open List, but covering the entire commission.

'Ch'   A rough muster, with only the muster letters and cheques set against each name.

'D'   A Description Book, containing a physical description and other details including place of residence and whether married, of each man.

'M'   A Monthly Muster , containing three months of fortnightly musters. The letter and number of a seaman's Register Ticket are entered (cf. the records of the General Register Office of Seamen, BT 112, 113, 114, & 116).

'O'   An Open List extended over four years.

Most of these musters in the new form contain alphabets.

ADM 41

These musters are of a special simplified form, including descriptions, for Hired Armed Vessels and Cutters during the Napoleonic Wars. Some of the musters are in fact on ordinary muster forms. The peculiarity of these vessels is that they were hired into naval service complete with their crews, who thus came under naval discipline though they had not entered for the Navy. The musters of vessels hired in earlier wars are among those of the regular men of war.

ADM 38

This class contains various strays from ADM 36 & 37, but chiefly consists of musters of the 1858 'New System', which replaced that used since the 1830s, but did not differ greatly from it. The following categories are distinguished:

'C'   Complete Books, including alphabet, covering the whole commission. The type and length of engagement is specified.

'D'   Description Book. There is a column for an 'Abstract of certificates Produced' which in effect provides a summary record of service.

'M'   A Quarterly Muster. The muster columns show no letters, but are left blank unless the man was chequed.

'O'   Open List, as before.

'V'   Victualling List, including various financial details not in other musters.

ADM 115

Although called Record & Establishment Books, this class in fact consists of a combination of Muster and Pay Book, concentrating on financial matters and containing no descriptions or records of certificates. By the time this pattern was introduced most men were on Continuous Service, and their C.S. numbers are entered, by which their Service records can readily be traced. Exact dates of birth are given.

ADM 117

This class contains the surviving Quarterly Ledgers, which in 1873 replaced the books of the 1858 system (ADM 38 & 115). These ledgers are combined musters and pay books closely resembling those ADM 115 which they superseded. Almost all of these ledgers later than 1878 were destroyed by enemy action in 1941.

ADM 119

Quarterly musters of Revenue Cruisers, 1824-1857, during which period they were under Admiralty control.

ADM 102

This class contains both hospital musters — that is, of the patients in naval hospitals, hospital ships and sick quarters — and pay lists of hospital staff. Musters for RNH Malta, 1804-1895, are in ADM 304/14-18, 21-24 and 36-41. Sick Quarters musters, 1757-1758, are in ADM 30/51-52, and Sick Quarters Arrears Lists, 1739-42, in ADM 30/6.

Pay Books

Besides the musters returned at intervals to the Clerk of the Cheque at his home yard, a captain was required in the eighteenth century to send five copies of a Pay Book to the Navy Office, with three alphabets, a Slop Book, Tobacco List, Sick List, List of Venereal Cures, the counterfoils of any tickets issued on board and other supporting documents. Two of these Pay Books went to the Controller's Office and the Navy Pay Office, the latter of which, as we shall see, made many payments on the books by the authority of the former. All these payments had to be entered in a Pay Book returned to the Clerk of the Cheque before the ship could be paid. The Pay Books therefore contain not only the original transcription of the Muster, but a variety of later entries in other hands.

Covers

The front covers of the Pay Books usually bear various notes, totals and rough working by the clerks, representing the successive stages of making up the completed book. These notes refer to the same figures as are entered within, and need not be explained separately.

The back cover of each book bears a formal note of the ship's name, the dates covered by the book, the date the ship was paid and who was present at the pay. The first name is that of the Commissioner who by custom was almost always present (the Commissioner of the yard, in most cases, though some ships, especially those hired or lost, were paid at the Pay Office in London). Then there is a note of when the book was 'made up' completely, with every entry in it accounted for, and the name of the Treasurer of the Navy to whose accounts it pertained. The process of 'making up' a Pay Book was seldom complete until years after the ship had been paid, and a Treasurer's accounts could not be cleared until every Pay Book opened in his period of office had been thus closed. Finally there are the totals of pay, full and net.

Pay Book Columns

The pay Book opens in just the same way as a muster (omitting the muster table). A note is often added to the first page of the date of ending wages, and the period, in months, weeks and days covered by the book. The months are invariably lunar months of twenty-eight days each, by which all wages were paid.

Most of the columns are identical to those of the Musters (though not always printed in exactly the same order) and need no further explanation. These columns (No., Entry & Year, Appearance, Whence & Whether Prest or Not, Age Place & County of Birth, No & Letter of Ticket. Mens Names, Qualities, Straggling, Neglect, Slop Clothes, Venereals, Trusses, Cloathes in Sick Quarters, Dead Men's Cloaths, Beds, Date of Parties Order for Allotting Monthly Pay and Marine Necessaries (sometimes 'Necessaries' and 'Stoppages' distinguished) were filled up by copying—or by not bothering to copy—from the muster. Other columns were either filled in differently, or are peculiar to the Pay Books.

D, DD or R
Time of Discharge & Year
Whither or for What Reason
These three columns, which may be taken together, contain more information than that transcribed from the musters. Men who had been discharged from the ship during the currency of the Pay Book were not likely to be on board when she was later paid, and a variety of other means of payment were available, (see below, 'Means of Payment') each noted in this place.

Retrospective entries were made against the names of men who had left the ship after the period covered by the Pay Book, but before the ship had been paid. These entries are distinguishable not only by different hand and ink, but by the details of how, when and whither discharged being usually omitted. Their purpose was to insure that these men, no longer on board at the time of pay, received their wages by some other means. Retrospective entries to the opposite effect were set against men then on the musters whose 'R' had been taken off appeal to the Navy Board or the Commissioner of the yard.

In these columns, or any others conveniently blank, are entered notes of the fulfilment of the conditions which all officers had to satisfy on order to draw their wages, thus:

Captains & Lieutenants:
>'Instructions passed no imprest'
>(that is, no deductions from wages on account of irregularity in accounts, impropriety in issuing stores or drawing on the Navy).

Masters:
>'Journal and Log Book delivered'
>(the Master's evidence of his diligent performance of duty, accompanied by a certificate to the same purpose from the Captain).

Midshipmen & Master's Mates:
>'Journal produced'
>(not only evidence of duty performed in order to draw wages, but also in order to qualify to be examined for lieutenant).

Pursers:
>'Proper certificates produced'
>(certificates from the Captain, Agent Victualler and others of financial propriety, which allowed the Purser to draw his wages and allowances. Passing his accounts, which was of much greater financial importance to him, had to wait on the paying of the ship).

Carpenters, Boatswains, Surgeons & Gunners:
>'Accounts passed'
>(by the Navy Board for the first three, and by the Ordnance Board for the last).

Coopers, Stewards and Steward's Mates:
>'Purser's consent'
>(these ratings were in effect appointed personally by the Purser, whose approval was required for them to draw their wages).

Here also is noted, whenever warrant officers had been appointed during a commission, the confirmation of their warrants by the Navy Board (or the Ordnance Board in the case of Gunners and Armourers) without which they could not be paid in their new ranks.

It sometimes happened that a man's first entry in the muster was for some reason cancelled and a new entry made *de novo* elsewhere. These cases are usually noted in these columns as 'D to [the appropriate entry] with Original Entry and Charges', often abbreviated to OE &C.

If a man were discharged on the muster in circumstances which left his ultimate fate or whereabouts unknown, he was noted as Dq or Dsq, and the Q (for 'query') acted as a check to payment until removed from the Pay Book. Occasionally this was done by formal order, as with an R, but more often it was implicitly taken off by addition of subsequent information. In the case of men Dsq to hospital, which was by far the most common, one of five fates could befall them: they might be discharged dead, run, discharged unserviceable, discharged back to their ship and re-entered in the muster, or discharged into another ship. The first four are noted with the conventional abbreviations, the last as 'E' (entered) and the ship's name. With this information it was possible for the clerks to pay the men; without it their wages ought to have remained unpaid, though in fact the clerks did not always remember to enter the information which had allowed them to make payment.

Front of Ledger
In this column are entered deductions extraneous to the Pay Book proper, usually errors corrected from previous books.

Wages remitted from Aboard
As noted above under Musters, this column contained the sums remitted from overseas under the terms of the 1758 Navy Act. A remittance could be claimed by the designated recipient on proof of identity from any Clerk of the Cheque, Naval Officer, Collector of Customs or Receiver of Land Tax in Britain, and from 1759 in Ireland.

Three pence per £
Three pence in the pound was deducted from the officers' wages for the officers' widows' pension fund.

Wages remitted at the Pay of the Ship
The 1758 Navy Act required that ships in home waters were not to be more than six months in arrears of pay, and that at each pay the ship's company were to have the opportunity to make home remittances in the same way as those abroad. Entries in this column and that of Overseas Remittances are alternatives, since no ship could be in two places at once — though of course she could in the course of a commission.

Chest
Every officer and man was charged a shilling a month for the support of the Chatham Chest. Only sixpence, however, actually went to the Chest; fourpence went to the Chaplain and twopence to the Surgeon for their respective duties.

Hospital
Sixpence a month was deducted from every officer and man for Greenwich Hospital, as it was from merchant seamen.

Full Wages

The total pay due before deductions.

Solving Column

A narrow column without a heading. In this was set a mark ✗ to indicate 'paid'.

Neat Wages

The net pay after deductions. Remittances are totalled separately.

When Paid

The total is self-explanatory. No entry was made for the majority of men who were paid at the pay of the ship (the date of which is given on the back cover).

To Whom Paid

This column also assumes payment to the individual in cash at the pay of the ship, and notes only the variations from that rule. Here are entered not only the name of the recipient, but the method of payment (for which see below), and the recipients' relation to the payee. Recipients include not only kinsmen but attorneys, assignees, and the administrators or executors of wills. A high proportion of the wages due to non-members or former members of the ships' company was in fact received on their behalf by their attorneys or other agents, many of whom were the same clerks who attended in their official capacity. The names of Navy Agents, bankers and ticket-buyers also figure prominently. Since servants' wages were paid to their masters the entry against a servants' name is often 'as his master' or some such, and that for the officer qualified 'and for his servants'. For the same reason references to wives and mothers against servants' names are to the officers' womenfolk, not the boys'. All entries in this column are heavily abbreviated.

Means of Payment

By the late eighteenth century, there existed a variety of ways in which men could be paid, or transfer their pay, other than in cash at the pay of the ship. These methods were:

Assigned Tickets

Men could, with their captains' consent, assign their tickets by a legal instrument in favour of a named individual, usually a ticket broker or innkeeper. By this means the seamen were easily defrauded, and captains severely discouraged assignment, or forced the assignees to accept lower rates of discount when the tickets were presented for payment. Not all assignees, however, were ticket brokers, as the method could also be used to make over pay to relatives. Under the terms of the 1758 Navy Act all assignments of wages were void unless revocable at pleasure.

Remittances

The remittance system established by the 1758 Navy Act and the allotment system of the 1795 Navy Act have already been described. Since the recipient of the remittance and of the balance of pay were not necessarily, or even usually, the same person two entries were made in the 'To Whom Paid' column. Books of Remittance Lists of ships paid at Plymouth, 1758-1798, are in ADM 174/291-293. Remittance Lists 1795-1851 are in ADM 26, and Allotment Lists 1795-1852, in ADM 27.

Removed Lists

These lists, usually referred to simply as 'lists' or 'Pay Lists', but sometimes as 'Turn Over' Lists (TOL), were of men turned-over to other ships, and represented a transfer of credit from one ships' books to another, in order that a man might receive pay for his old ship on board his new. The 1758 Act made it obligatory to pay men on being turned-over, other than by request. Removed lists were also used to pay Marines discharged to barracks and paid by the Paymaster of Marines.

List of Officers

From 1747 Sea officers could draw their own and their servants' wages annually from the Navy Pay Office upon satisfying the conditions prescribed by the regulations, and a list of all such payments had to be received and entered into the Pay Book before the ship was paid. Officers' pay was almost always collected by Navy Agents, one of whose principal functions was passing the accounts and claiming the wages of their absent clients. The List of Officers is commonly abbreviated in the Pay Books to LO. It was important for the Treasurer's clerks to know in whose Treasurership the list had been paid—not usually the same as that in which the Pay Book was made up, nor necessarily the same as that in which the ship was paid—so the initials of the Treasurer were often added. This gives rise to entries abbreviated thus: 'pLOGGN2'; meaning, paid by list of officers in the second Treasurership of George Grenville. Successive lists were numbered. Lists of Officers for 1747 are in ADM 30/32.

Annual List

Another list, very like the former and including some officers, was made up of all those who had been discharged to hospital or elsewhere or paid by ticket, which might be cashed at any date before or after the ship was paid. These pays were charged to an Annual List ('AL'), likewise numbered and assigned to a specific treasurer.

Recalls

After the ship had been paid, tickets might be cashed or other payments made as long as the Pay Book remained open, which in the eighteenth century was often ten or twelve years. This was done on fixed days, usually once a month, known as 'recalls'. Pays made on recalls are entered in the Pay Book with those made at paying off. Examples of lists of pays due on recall are in ADM 30/17 (1674) and ADM 10/12 (1701).

Arrears Lists

There usually remained a few unclaimed pays when the Pay Book was made up, which were entered on a list of arrears for the Treasurer in question and transferred to his successor. Some Arrears Lists, 1689-1710, are in ADM 30/2-5.

Indentures

Apprentices, indentured servants and others made over all or part of their wages to their masters by indenture, which document, lodged in the Pay Office, entitled the master to draw the wages.

Bounty Lists

Under the provisions of various wartime Orders in Council, a bounty was payable to volunteers. This was not strictly part of pay, and not charged on the Pay Books, but on separate Bounty Lists which were referred to particular Treasurers in the same way as other lists for payment. Bounty Lists 1695-1708 and 1741-42 are in ADM 30/8-16, and a Bounty Recall List of 1674 in ADM 30/17.

Abstract

At the end of the Pay Book is a page on which the totals of each column made up at the foot of each page are themselves added to give overall figures for each column for the whole book. The total of all deductions subtracted from the full wages gives the net wages due at the pay of the ship, which the clerks carried on board in cash the day they came to pay her. A separate total is sometimes made of 'defalcations', by which is meant actual deductions from wages, as opposed to payments made by other means. The total of the Chest is always divided into the half actually due to the Chest, the Chaplain's fourpences and the Surgeon's twopences.

Receipts

Also at the end of the Pay Books are receipts signed in person, or more commonly by an agent, from the Chaplain for his fourpences, from the Surgeon for his twopences and his fees for venereal cures, from the Purser for his tobacco money, and from the slop contractor (before 1758) or any sea or naval officer who might have provided slops.

Pay Book Alphabets

These are indexes to the Pay Books in order of initial letter of surname only, and are generally to be found bound in with the Ticket Office Pay Books (ADM 32) and in the Treasurer's Pay Books (ADM 33) from about 1765. Later classes all have alphabets.

Enclosures

Loose in the pages of the Pay Books (particularly ADM 32 & 33) are slop lists, tobacco lists and other documents returned with them, besides some correspondence with the Pay Office. In the seventeenth century Pay Books in ADM 33 are also some officers' commissions, warrants and certificates of passing their accounts.

Pay Book Classes

ADM 31
A single bundle of Controller's Pay Books selected to make up gaps in other series. They differ in no material respect from the other classes.

ADM 32
Ticket Office Pay Books selected to make up the deficiencies in the Treasurer's Pay Books, which they exactly resemble.

ADM 33
The first series of Treasurer's Pay Books, including the earliest survivals from the 1660s, which are of a somewhat simpler and more primitive pattern than those of a century later but not essentially different from them. In some Pay Books of the 1670s addresses have been entered in the 'To Whom Paid' column.

ADM 34
The second series of Treasurer's Pay Books, indistinguishable from the first which it overlaps in date. It is listed in the order in which the books are bound up, with initial letters together, but not in alphabetical order. Ships' names of two or more words are generally listed in two places, thus: *Charming Nancy* under both C and N, *Hearts of Oak* under both H and O. The enquirer should look under both names, as the list is not completely consistent and the binding policy was erratic.

ADM 35
The third series of Treasurer's Pay Books, indistinguishable from either of the others, and overlapping both. In the latter pieces of the class there are some minor changes from those of the previous century. This class also is listed in the old style.

ADM 115 & 117
See under Musters above.

Tracing Individuals

It will be obvious that an individual (other than a sea officer) can only be located in a Muster or Pay Book if his ship be known, but if it be known, his career both earlier and later can in certain circumstances be traced through successive musters. The chief difficulty in doing so arises from the fact that, until the introduction of Continuous Service from 1853, men entered only for a particular commission in a particular ship, and there was no legal or practical reason why they should at once enter one man of war on discharge from another. During the seventeenth and eighteenth centuries seamen moved easily between the King's and the merchants' service, and there is no certainty that the men of a warship paying off in peace time would re-enter the Navy later. In practice a considerable proportion would, especially petty officers and seamen of long service in the Navy. They were most likely, though by no means certain, to enter in another ship commissioning, or otherwise recruiting, at the same port and not more than a couple of months after they had been paid off. Even if they did so enter, however, it may be necessary to search the musters of many ships to find them. In the nineteenth century the seamen of the Navy became somewhat of a closed, and even hereditary caste, mingling relatively little with merchant seamen, and therefore very likely to enter the Service soon after paying off. To this end the Admiralty always tried to commission a ship at any port where another had just paid off, and as the number of ships in commission was for most of the century extremely small, it is much easier to trace a man from one to another.

In wartime, men were usually turned over directly from one ship to another, which of course makes it easier to trace an individual's service, but there remain many difficulties. It is essential to search all the lists of a muster, as men newly turned-over are likely to be entered first as supernumeraries. Men lent in lieu or given leave easily became separated from their ships and were borne as supernumeraries in the guard ship while being lent to a succession of tenders and other vessels. Men sent ashore to Sick Quarters were also very likely to be left behind, and before 1756 were sometimes borne on the books of ship which they had not seen for years. From 1756 they were supposed to be discharged onto the hospital's books (ADM 102, Hospital Musters), thence to the guard ship, so back to their old ship or to some other. Men given leave when ships paid off in wartime were sometimes instructed to report back to a given ship, even in another port, which instructions be usually be found only in Admiralty In-letters and Orders (ADM 1 & 2). One important fact which may often provide the clue to the career to a seaman, especially in the eighteenth century, is the existence of followings. Most officers, especially Captains and Admirals, had junior officers and men who followed them from ship to ship, often for many years. If the pattern of a man's entries and discharges suggests that he was following a particular officer, that officer's career may be used to help trace his followers.

For many purposes Musters and Pay Books may be treated as duplicates, and either series used to supply gaps in the other. It should be remembered, however, that many of the columns were copied from Masters to Pay Books and that any process of copying always introduces errors and omissions. On the other hand the Pay Books contain alphabets at least fifty years before the Musters, and they include many entries, especially in the 'To Whom Paid' column, stating or implying information about next of kin. Retrospective entries in the Pay Books against the names of men discharged, especially the re-entries of men discharged cured from hospital, can often provide a link in a man's career not given by the Musters.

Nevertheless, the task of tracing individual men in the Musters and Pay Books, though it can be lightened by experience, remains a difficult and laborious one with many pitfalls. The documents were never intended for such purposes, and are not well adapted to them.

APPENDIX I

Analysis of Service Records

This appendix contains all the records dealt with in this book, arranged under the standard types defined in Chapter Three, and in chronological order within each type. Some records of a varied or indeterminate character have been entered under more than one type. Those which are listed in a Series are described in more detail in Appendix II.

The ranks and ratings are as described in Chapter Two, and must be understood as including changes of title and creation of new ranks according to date, so that 'Lieutenants' include Lieutenant-Commanders from 1914, 'Masters' include the Navigating Branch, and 'Chaplains' include Naval Instructors.

1 Analyses

	PRO References	Dates	Remarks	Series
Surgeons	ADM 11/40	c1808		
Master's Assistants, Clerks	ADM 1/5123/15	1835		
Boatswains, Gunners, Carpenters	ADM 1/5123/16	1836		
Flag Officers, Captains, Commanders, Lieutenants	ADM 11/64	1844		
Lieutenants	ADM 6/174	1847		
Flag Officers, Captains, Commanders, Lieutenants	ADM 11/10	1848		
Flag Officers, Captains, Commanders, Lieutenants	ADM 11/80	1893-1900		

2 Applications

	PRO References	Dates	Remarks	Series
Captains, Lieutenants, Pursers, Boatswains, Gunners, Carpenters, Cooks	ADM 6/428	1673-1689		
Pursers, Boatswains, Gunners, Carpenters	ADM 6/187-189	1770-1795		A
Chaplains	ADM 6/188-189	1783-1795		A
Lieutenants	ADM 6/170-172	1799-1818		
Captains, Commanders, Lieutenants, Boatswains, Carpenters, Chaplains	ADM 6/212	1801-1803	To be superseded	B
Poor Knights of Windsor	ADM 106/3535	1812-1821		
Boatswains, Gunners, Carpenters	ADM 6/190	1818-1820		

2 Applications contd

	PRO References	Dates	Remarks	Series
GH Nurses	ADM 6/331	1819-1842		
Ratings	ADM 175/74-81	1819-1866	For Coast Guard	C
Masters	ADM 106/3518	1823-1831		
Surgeons	ADM 6/186	1829-1833	Convict Ships	
Ratings	ADM 6/199	1831-1850	For Coast Guard	
Flag Officers, Captains, Commanders, Lieutenants, Masters, Pursers, Yard Officers	ADM 6/1-2	1842-1858		
Boatswains, Gunners, Carpenters, Chaplains	ADM 6/1	1842-1858		
Surgeons	ADM 6/2	1844-1850		

3 Appointments

	PRO References	Dates	Remarks	Series
Captains, Commanders, Lieutenants	ADM 30/34	1793-1800	Impress Service	
Captains, Commanders, Lieutenants	ADM 28/145	1798-1801	Sea Fencibles	
Captains, Commanders, Lieutenants	ADM 28/145	1803-1810	Sea Fencibles	
Captains, Commanders, Lieutenants	ADM 11/18	1803-1815		
Lieutenants	ADM 6/55	1803-1807		
Captains, Commanders, Lieutenants	ADM 11/14-17	1804-1815		D
Mates, Sub-Lieutenants	ADM 11/19	1805-1810	Sub-Lieutenants	
Midshipmen, Ratings	ADM 30/53-54	1810-1816	Signal Stations	
Lieutenants, Midshipmen, Ratings	ADM 7/591	c1810-1814	Signal Stations	
Lieutenants, Masters, Boatswains	ADM 6/56	1816-1831	Revenue Cruizers	
Lieutenants, Masters, Boatswains	ADM 2/1127	1822-1832	Revenue Cruizers	

	PRO References	Dates	Remarks	Series
3 Appointments contd				
Foreign Officers	ADM 11/27-30	1830-1853		E
Ratings	ADM 6/199	1831-1850	Coast Guard Boatmen	
Foreign Officers	ADM 11/81	1853-1858		E
4 Black Books				
Masters, Surgeons, Pursers, Boatswains, Gunners, Carpenters, Chaplains	ADM 11/39	1741-1814		F
Captains, Commanders, Lieutenants	ADM 12/27B-27E	1759-1815		
Captains, Commanders, Lieutenants	ADM 12/27A	1810-1816	Court Martial convictions	
Master's Assistants	ADM 11/27-29	1826-1839		
Mates, Midshipmen	ADM 11/27-29	1830-1848		
Captains, Engineers	ADM 11/49	1835-1842		
Captains, Commanders, Lieutenants	ADM 6/445	1846-1872		
5 Commissions				
Flag Officers, Captains, Commanders Lieutenants	ADM 6/3-32	1695-1815		G
Captains, Commanders, Lieutenants	ADM 10/13	1730-1818	Navy Office fee books	
Captains, Commanders, Lieutenants	ADM 1/5115/10	1742	Mediterranean	
Captains, Commanders	ADM 6/61	1742-1768	Abroad	

5 Commissions contd

	PRO References	Dates	Remarks	Series
Lieutenants	ADM 6/62	1742-1768	Abroad	
Flag Officers, Captains, Commanders, Lieutenants	ADM 6/33-38	1744-1798	Admiralty fee books, outports	H
Captains, Commanders, Lieutenants	ADM 1/5116/12	1757-1770	North America and West Indies	
Captains, Commanders, Lieutenants	ADM 1/5117/1	1769-1773	West Indies	
Captains, Commanders, Lieutenants	ADM 7/761	1779-1784	East Indies	
Captains, Commanders, Lieutenants	ADM 6/64-65	1787-1805	Abroad	
Captains, Commanders, Lieutenants	ADM 6/54	1795-1815	From Half-Pay	
Captains, Commanders, Lieutenants	ADM 6/46-47	1802-1827	Admiralty fee books, outports	H
Captains, Commanders, Lieutenants, Mates, Sub-Lieutenants	ADM 6/53	1804-1806		
Captains, Commanders, Lieutenants	ADM 7/558	1807-1809	Abroad	
Captains, Commanders, Lieutenants	ADM 7/558	1814-1815	Abroad	
Captains, Commanders, Lieutenants	ADM 6/68-72	1824-1846	Abroad	
Flag Officers, Captains, Commanders, Lieutenants	ADM 6/48-49	1832-1849	Admiralty fee books, outports	H
Flag Officers	ADM 7/919	1860-1870	C-in-C	
Sub-Lieutenants	ADM 11/22	1860-1865		I
Sub-Lieutenants	ADM 11/89	1865-1880		I

6 Candidates for Promotion

	PRO References	Dates	Remarks	Series
Cadets	ADM 11/53	1811-1836	For RNC	

6 Candidates for Promotion contd

	PRO References	Dates	Remarks	Series
Cadets	ADM 7/1	1813-1835	For RNC	J
Lieutenants, Masters	ADM 6/180	1814-1816		J
Mates, Midshipmen	ADM 6/176-180	1814-1816		K
Surgeons	ADM 105/1-9	1817-1832	Victualling Board submissions	
Coast Guard Officers & Ratings	ADM 175/74-81	1819-1866	Nominations	C
Masters	ADM 106/3517	1820-1825		
Coast Guard Officers & Ratings	ADM 175/99-100	1821-1849	Nominations, Ireland	
Surgeons	ADM 105/10-19	1822-1832		AK
Armourers	WO 54/881-882	1827-1838	Applications for	
Pursers, Boatswains, Gunners, Carpenters	ADM 11/38	1828		
Mates, Sub-Lieutenants	ADM 6/198	1830		
Coast Guard Ratings	ADM 6/199	1831-1850	Nominations of RN ratings	
Surgeons	ADM 105/37-39	1838-1866	MDG's submissions	
Master's Assistants	ADM 11/21	1839-1849		
Captains, Commanders, Lieutenants	ADM 11/1	c1841-1861		
Mates, Sub-Lieutenants	ADM 6/181	1845-1853		
Cadets	ADM 11/30	1848-1852	Board nominations	
Coast Guard Ratings	ADM 175/101	1851-1856	Nominations of RN ratings	
Surgeons	ADM 104/45-50	1854-1926	MDG's submissions	L
Pursers	ADM 11/45	1856		

6 Candidates for Promotion contd

	PRO References	Dates	Remarks	Series
Pursers	ADM 11/46	1856	Asst. Paymasters	
Lieutenants	ADM 196/69-70	1861		
Cadets	ADM 6/447	1869-1871	For nominations	
Surgeons	ADM 6/468	1870-1902	For Surgeon. Physical Exams.	
Commanders	ADM 7/929	c1879-1895	(Seniority to 1855 only)	
Commanders	ADM 7/930	c1879-1895	(Seniority to 1895 only)	
Cadets	ADM 6/448-451	1882-1905	Service Nominations	M
Cadets	ADM 6/464-467	1898-1917	For nominations	N

7 Certificates of Service

	PRO References	Dates	Remarks	Series
Mates, Midshipmen	ADM 6/86-118	1744-1819	Passing for Lieutenant	O
Ratings	ADM 73/1-35	1790-1865	For Greenwich Hospital	P
Masters	ADM 6/135-168	c1800-1850		Q
Mates, Sub-Lieutenants	ADM 107/71-75	1802-1848	Candidates for Lieutenant	R
Masters, Surgeons, Pursers, Boatswains, Gunners, Carpenters, Chaplains, Cooks, Shipwrights	ADM 29/1	1802-1814	For Superannuation	
Pursers, Boatswains, Gunners, Carpenters	ADM 6/121	1803-1804	Candidates	

7 Certificates of Service contd

	PRO References	Dates	Remarks	Series
Gunners	ADM 6/128	1803-1805	On passing	
Ratings	ADM 29/2	1803-1816		
Mates, Midshipmen	ADM 6/182	1814		
Surgeons	ADM 104/30	1815-1822		
Boatswains	ADM 29/4	1817-1839	For Pension	S
Gunners	ADM 29/3	1817-1839	For Pension	T
Carpenters	ADM 29/5-6	1817-1853	For Pension	U
Cooks	ADM 29/5	1817-1833	For Pension	
Artificers	ADM 29/8	1817-1845		
Chaplains	ADM 11/41	1833-1834		
Cooks	ADM 29/7	1834-1851	For Pension	
Ratings	ADM 29/9-22	1834-1840		V, W
Boatswains	ADM 29/23	1840-1870	For Pension	S
Gunners	ADM 29/24	1840-1871	For Pension	T
Ratings	ADM 29/25-96	1840-1894		V, W
Mates, Sub-Lieutenants	ADM 11/88	1847-1854	Candidates for Lieutenant	
Masters, Pursers	ADM 11/88	1847-1854	Candidates	
Engineers	ADM 29/112	1870-1873	For Pension	
Boatswains, Gunners, Carpenters	ADM 29/121	1870-1873	For Pension	S, T, U

8 Confidential Reports

	PRO References	Dates	Remarks	Series
Gunners	ADM 6/462	1881-1900		
Nursing Sisters	ADM 104/95	1890-1908		

8 Confidential Reports contd

	PRO References	Dates	Remarks	Series
Flag Officers, Captains	ADM 196/86-94	1893-1944	(Seniority)	EU
Flag Officers, Captains	ADM 203/99	1904-1914	War Course	

9 Disposition Lists

	PRO References	Dates	Remarks	Series
Lieutenants	ADM 8/1-95	1673-1808		ES
Flag Officers, Captains, Commanders	ADM 8/1-100	1673-1813		ES
Mates, Midshipmen, Cadets	ADM 6/183	1849		
Gunners	ADM 6/463	1893-1924		
Flag Officers, Captains, Commanders, Lieutenants, Mates, Sub-Lieutenants, Midshipmen, Surgeons, Pursers, Engineers, Boatswains, Gunners, Carpenters, Chaplains, all Wt & Cd. Wt. Officers	ADM 177/1-18	1914-1918	+ Other Navy Lists	X
Surgeons	ADM 104/44	1914-1916	Temp. Surgeons	
WRNS Officers	ADM 321/1-2	1917-1919		
Flag Officers, Captains, Commanders, Lieutenants, Sub-Lieutenants, Midshipmen, Surgeons, Pursers, Engineers, Boatswains, Gunners, Carpenters, Chaplains, all Wt. & Cd. Wt. Officers	ADM 177/19-61	1939-1945	+ Other Navy Lists	X

10 Examinations

	PRO References	Dates	Remarks	Series
Cadets	ADM 6/119	1816-1818	RNC Navigation & Maths	
Mates, Sub-Lieutenants	ADM 11/22	1829-1865	Passing for Lieutenant	I
Captains, Commanders, Lieutenants, Mates, Sub-Lieutenants	ADM 6/60	1841-1842	(Compiled) Gunnery Qualifications	
Mates, Sub-Lieutenants	ADM 11/89	1865-1880	Passing for Lieutenant	I
Captains, Commanders, Lieutenants, Engineers, Constructors	ADM 203/21-44	1876-1957	RNC Greenwich	Y
Masters	ADM 203/40	1876-1880	RNC Greenwich	Y
Cadets, Assistant Clerks, Probationer Constructors, Schoolmasters, Yard Officers	CSC 10	1876-1991		FB
Cadets	ADM 6/469-473	1877-1902	*Britannia* Final Exams	Z
Masters	ADM 203/21-27	1880-1886	RNC Greenwich	Y
Surgeons	ADM 305/71-72	1884-1914	RN Medical School	
Engineer & Constructor Cadets	ADM 7/931	1897-1909	RNEC Keyham	
Sub-Lieutenants	ADM 203/41-44	1907-1957	RNC Greenwich	Y
Naval Instructors	ADM 203/42-44	1920-1957	RNC Greenwich	Y

11 Honours and Awards

	PRO References	Dates	Remarks	Series
Flag Officers, Captains, Commanders, Lieutenants, Midshipmen	ADM 7/706	1793-1807		

11 Honours and Awards contd

	PRO References	Dates	Remarks	Series
Flag Officers, Captains, Commanders, Lieutenants, Mates, Sub-Lieutenants, Midshipmen, Masters, Surgeons, Pursers, Chaplains, Engineers, Boatswains, Gunners, Carpenters, Ratings	ADM 171/1-77	1793-1952	Medal Rolls	EV
Flag Officers, Captains, Commanders, Lieutenants, Mates, Sub-Lieutenants, Midshipmen, Masters, Surgeons, Pursers, Chaplains, Engineers, Boatswains, Gunners, Carpenters, Ratings	ADM 171/89-166	1793-1972	Medal Rolls	EV
Flag Officers, Captains, Commanders, Lieutenants, Mates, Masters, Surgeons, Pursers, Engineers, Boatswains, Gunners, Carpenters	ADM 11/51-52	1833-1846		
Flag Officers, Captains, Commanders, Lieutenants, Mates, Sub-Lieutenants, Masters, Surgeons, Pursers, Engineers, Boatswains, Gunners, Carpenters, Chaplains, Coast Guard Officers, Ratings	ADM 7/912	1852-1898		
Flag Officers, Captains, Commanders, Lieutenants, Mates, Sub-Lieutenants, Midshipmen, Surgeons, Pursers, Chaplains, Engineers, Boatswains, Gunners, Carpenters, other WO	ADM 171/78-88	1914-1919		EW

	PRO References	Dates	Remarks	Series
11 Honours and Awards contd				
Cd. & Wt. Officers, inc. RM, RNR, RNVR, RNAS, WRNS, QARNNS	ADM 171/172	1916-1921	Foreign decorations	
RNR Officers	BT 164/23	1939-1946		
12 Leave Books				
Captains, Lieutenants	ADM 106/2972	1762-1777		
Flag Officers, Captains, Commanders, Lieutenants, Masters, Surgeons, Pursers, Boatswains, Gunners, Carpenters, Chaplains	ADM 6/207-211	1783-1847	Abroad	AA
Flag Officers, Captains, Commanders, Lieutenants, Masters, Surgeons, Pursers, Boatswains, Gunners, Carpenters, Chaplains, Yard Officers	ADM 6/200-205	1804-1846		AB
Flag Officers, Captains, Commanders, Lieutenants, Masters, Surgeons, Pursers, Boatswains, Gunners, Carpenters, Chaplains, Yard Officers	ADM 6/206	1809-1812		
13 Marriage Certificates				
Flag Officers, Captains, Commanders, Lieutenants, Masters, Surgeons Pursers, Boatswains, Gunners, Carpenters	ADM 30/57	1801-1818	Claimants for Pension	

13 Marriage Certificates contd

	PRO References	Dates	Remarks	Series
Flag Officers, Captains, Commanders, Lieutenants, Masters, Surgeons, Pursers, Engineers, Chaplains	ADM 13/70-71	1806-1866		AC
Flag Officers, Captains, Commanders, Lieutenants, Masters, Surgeons, Pursers, Engineers, Chaplains	ADM 13/186-192	1866-1902		AC
Boatswains, Gunners, Carpenters	ADM 13/191-192	c1891-1902		AC

14 Casualty Records

	PRO References	Dates	Remarks	Series
Captains, Commanders, Lieutenants, Mates, Sub-Lieutenants, Midshipmen, Cadets, Masters, Surgeons, Pursers, Boatswains, Gunners, Carpenters, Chaplains, Cooks, Masters at Arms, Ratings	ADM 106/3017-3035	1675-1822	Bounty to next-of-kin	AD, AE
Captains, Commanders, Lieutenants, Mates, Sub-Lieutenants, Midshipmen, Cadets, Masters, Surgeons, Pursers, Boatswains, Gunners, Carpenters, Chaplains, Cooks, Masters at Arms, Ratings	ADM 30/20	1795-1832	Bounty to next-of-kin	
Ratings	ADM 141	1802-1861		
Flag Officers, Captains, Commanders, Lieutenants, Masters, Surgeons, Pursers, Boatswains, Gunners, Carpenters, Chaplains	ADM 11/51-52	1833-1846		AF

14 Casualty Records *contd*

	PRO References	Dates	Remarks	Series
Flag Officers, Captains, Commanders, Lieutenants, Mates, Sub-Lieutenants, Midshipmen, Cadets, Surgeons, Pursers, Engineers, Boatswains, Gunners, Carpenters, Chaplains, other Wt. & Cd. Wt. Officers	ADM 6/445	1846-1872		
Ratings	ADM 104/144-149	1854-1929		FA
Ratings	ADM 154	1859-1878		AF
Flag Officers, Captains, Commanders, Lieutenants, Mates, Sub-Lieutenants, Midshipmen, Cadets, Surgeons, Pursers, Engineers, Boatswains, Gunners, Carpenters, Chaplains, other Wt. & Cd. Wt. Officers / Ratings	ADM 104/109-121	1893-1956	Deaths other than by enemy action	EX
All Officers & Ratings	ADM 116/529	1899-1900	Naval Brigade, S. Africa	
Ratings	ADM 104/122-126	1900-1941	Enemy action	EY
All Cd. & Wt. Officers inc RNR, RNVR, RNAS & CG	ADM 10/16	1903-1933	Inc. dismissals & resignations	
Flag Officers, Captains, Commanders, Lieutenants, Mates, Sub-Lieutenants, Midshipmen, Cadets, Surgeons, Pursers, Engineers, Boatswains, Gunners, Carpenters, Chaplains, other Wt. & Cd. Wt. Officers	ADM 242	1914-1920		AG, AH

14 Casualty Records contd

	PRO References	Dates	Remarks	Series
Surgeons	ADM 261/1	1939-1945		
RNR Officers	BT 164/23	1939-1946		
Ratings	ADM 104/127-139	1939-1948	Also prisoners of war	EZ

15 Half Pay

	PRO References	Dates	Remarks	Series
Flag Officers, Flag Captains	ADM 18/44-67	1668-1689		AI
Captains & Masters of 1st Rates	ADM 18/54-67	1674-1688		AI
Commodores	ADM 18/55-67	1675-1689		AI
Flag Officers, Captains, Lieutenants, Masters	ADM 25/1-255	1697-1836		AI
Captains	ADM 106/2970-2971	1704-1710		
Lieutenants	ADM 106/2970-2971	1705-1710		
Commanders	ADM 25/9-255	1715-1836		AI
Surgeons	ADM 25/24-255	1729-1836		AI
Flag Officers, Captains, Commanders, Lieutenants	ADM 6/213-219	1774-1800	Entitlement	AJ
Flag Officers, Captains, Commanders, Lieutenants, Masters, Surgeons	ADM 104/4-5	1778-1780	Entitlement	
Pursers	ADM 25/166-255	1814-1836		AI
Surgeons	ADM 105/1-9	1817-1832	Decisions & precedents	K
Chaplains	ADM 25/177-255	1817-1836		AI
Masters	ADM 11/5	1819-1822	Analysis of List	

15 Half Pay contd

	PRO References	Dates	Remarks	Series
Surgeons	ADM 105/10-19	1822-1832	Decisions & precedents	AK
Masters	ADM 11/4	c1831	Analysis of List	
Captains, Commanders, Lieutenants, Masters, Surgeons, Pursers, Chaplains	ADM 6/220-221	1834-1845	Entitlement	
Flag Officers, Captains, Commanders, Lieutenants, Masters, Surgeons, Pursers, Chaplains	PMG 15/1-3	1836-1858		AI
Flag Officers, Captains, Commanders	PMG 15/5	1838-1840		AI
Lieutenants	PMG 15/6	1838-1840		AI
Masters, Surgeons, Pursers	PMG 15/7	1838-1840		AI
Chaplains	PMG 15/6	1838-1840		AI
Flag Officers, Captains, Commanders, Lieutenants, Mates, Masters, Surgeons, Pursers, Chaplains	PMG 15/9-13	1840-1843		AI
Flag Officers, Captains, Commanders, Lieutenants, Mates, Masters, Surgeons, Pursers, Chaplains	PMG 15/15-19	1843-1846		AI
Flag Officers, Captains, Commanders, Lieutenants, Mates, Masters, Surgeons, Pursers, Chaplains	ADM 25/256	1846-1849		
Flag Officers, Captains, Commanders, Lieutenants, Mates, Masters, Surgeons, Pursers, Chaplains	PMG 15/21-25	1846-1849		AI
Masters	ADM 11/6	1847	Analysis of List	

15 Half Pay contd

	PRO References	Dates	Remarks	Series
Flag Officers, Captains, Commanders, Lieutenants, Mates, Sub-Lieutenants, Masters, Surgeons, Pursers, Chaplains	PMG 15/27-69	1849-1873		AI
Flag Officers, Captains, Commanders, Lieutenants, Masters	ADM 25/257	1851-1869	(Commencing)	
Engineers	PMG 15/37-69	1856-1873		AI
Flag Officers, Captains Commanders	ADM 25/259-260	1858-1886		
Surgeons	ADM 25/258	1858-1883		
Engineers	ADM 25/258	1865-1883		
Flag Officers, Captains, Commanders, Lieutenants, Masters, Surgeons, Pursers, Engineers, Boatswains, Gunners, Carpenters, Chaplains	ADM 23/33-34	1867-1871		AL
Flag Officers, Captains, Commanders, Lieutenants, Masters, Surgeons, Pursers, Engineers, Boatswains, Gunners, Carpenters, Chaplains	ADM 23/36-41	1871-1881		AL
Flag Officers, Captains, Commanders, Lieutenants, Sub-Lieutenants, Masters, Surgeons, Pursers, Engineers, Chaplains	PMG 15/75-78	1873-1876		AI
Flag Officers, Captains, Commanders, Lieutenants, Sub-Lieutenants, Masters, Surgeons, Pursers, Engineers, Chaplains	PMG 15/84-87	1876-1879		AI

15 Half Pay contd

	PRO References	Dates	Remarks	Series
Flag Officers, Captains, Commanders, Lieutenants, Sub-Lieutenants, Masters, Surgeons, Pursers, Engineers, Chaplains	PMG 15/93-96	1879-1882		AI
Flag Officers, Captains, Commanders, Lieutenants, Masters, Surgeons, Pursers, Engineers, Chaplains	ADM 23/125-140	1881-1900		AL
Flag Officers, Captains, Commanders, Lieutenants, Sub-Lieutenants, Masters, Surgeons, Pursers, Engineers, Chaplains	PMG 15/102-105	1882-1885		AI
Lieutenants, Sub-Lieutenants	ADM 25/261	1883-1886		
Masters, Pursers, Engineers	ADM 25/262	1883-1886		
Surgeons, Chaplains	ADM 25/263	1883-1886		
Flag Officers, Captains, Commanders, Lieutenants, Sub-Lieutenants, Masters, Surgeons, Pursers, Engineers, Chaplains	PMG 15/111-114	1885-1888		AI
Flag Officers, Captains, Commanders, Lieutenants, Sub-Lieutenants, Masters, Surgeons, Pursers, Engineers, Chaplains	PMG 15/120-123	1888-1892		AI
Flag Officers, Captains, Commanders, Lieutenants, Mates, Sub-Lieutenants, Masters, Surgeons, Pursers, Engineers, Chaplains	PMG 15/129-148	1892-1912		AI

15 Half Pay contd

	PRO References	Dates	Remarks	Series
Flag Officers, Captains, Commanders, Lieutenants, Mates, Sub-Lieutenants, Midshipmen, Masters, Surgeons, Pursers, Engineers, Chaplains	ADM 25/264-276	1900-1924		AL
Flag Officers, Captains, Commanders, Lieutenants, Mates, Sub-Lieutenants, Masters, Surgeons, Pursers, Engineers, Chaplains	PMG 15/178-182	1912-1920		AI

16 Pensions to Widows and Orphans

	PRO References	Dates	Remarks	Series
Midshipmen, Masters, Pursers, Boatswains, Gunners, Carpenters, Chaplains, Cooks, Ratings	ADM 82/1-2	1653-1657	Chatham Chest	
All Officers & Ratings	SP 18/63, 119, 151, 177	1653-1657	Sick & Hurt Board recommendations	
Flag Officers, Captains, Commanders, Lieutenants	ADM 18/53-118	1673-1781	Admiralty Pensions	AM
Midshipmen, Masters, Surgeons, Boatswains, Gunners, Carpenters, Cooks, Ratings	ADM 82/12-119	1675-1799	Chatham Chest	AN
Flag Officers, Captains, Commanders, Lieutenants, Pilots	ADM 7/809-814	1689-1785	Admiralty Pensions	AO
Flag Officers, Captains, Commanders, Lieutenants, Pilots	ADM 181/1-27	1707-1818	Admiralty Pensions	EM

16 Pensions to Widows and Orphans contd

	PRO References	Dates	Remarks	Series
Flag Officers, Captains, Commanders, Lieutenants, Masters, Surgeons, Pursers, Boatswains, Gunners, Carpenters	ADM 6/332-334	1732-1829	Minutes	AP
Flag Officers, Captains, Commanders, Lieutenants, Masters, Surgeons, Pursers, Boatswains, Gunners, Carpenters	ADM 22/56-237	1734-1835		AQ
Flag Officers, Captains, Commanders, Lieutenants, Pilots	ADM 22/1-5	1781-1793	Admiralty Pensions	AM
Flag Officers, Captains, Commanders, Lieutenants, Pilots	ADM 22/17-30	1793-1821	Admiralty Pensions	AM
Flag Officers, Captains, Commanders, Lieutenants, Masters, Surgeons, Pursers, Boatswains, Gunners, Carpenters	ADM 6/335-384	1797-1829		AR
Flag Officers, Captains, Commanders, Lieutenants, Pilots	ADM 22/51	1807-1809	Admiralty Pensions	
Flag Officers, Captains, Commanders, Lieutenants, Masters, Surgeons, Pursers, Boatswains, Gunners, Carpenters	ADM 6/385-402	1808-1830	Doubtful cases	AS
Flag Officers, Captains, Commanders, Lieutenants, Masters, Surgeons, Pursers	ADM 6/323-328	1809-1836	Compassionate Fund	AT

16 Pensions to Widows and Orphans contd

	PRO References	Dates	Remarks	Series
Flag Officers, Captains, Commanders, Lieutenants, Masters, Surgeons, Pursers, Boatswains, Gunners, Carpenters	ADM 22/238	1809-1820	Applications	
Flag Officers, Captains, Commanders, Lieutenants, Masters, Surgeons	ADM 22/239-252	1809-1851	Compassionate Fund	AU
Flag Officers, Captains, Commanders, Lieutenants, Pilots	ADM 22/31-36	1818-1828	Admiralty Pensions	AV
Flag Officers, Captains, Commanders, Lieutenants, Masters, Surgeons, Pursers, Boatswains, Gunners, Carpenters	ADM 6/330	1819-1829		
Flag Officers, Captains, Commanders, Lieutenants, Pilots	ADM 22/39-46	1828-1832	Admiralty Pensions, outports	AW
Flag Officers, Captains, Commanders, Lieutenants, Masters, Surgeons, Pursers, Boatswains, Gunners, Carpenters, Chaplains, Coast Guard Officers	ADM 23/106-107	1830-1878		
Flag Officers, Captains, Commanders, Lieutenants, Masters, Surgeons, Pursers, Boatswains, Gunners, Carpenters	ADM 23/22	1830-1833	Admiralty Pensions	
Flag Officers, Captains, Commanders, Lieutenants, Masters, Surgeons	ADM 22/253	1830-1832	Compassionate Fund, outports	
Gunners, Boatswains, Carpenters, Cooks, Yard Officers, Artificers, Pilots, Ratings	ADM 22/52-55	1831-1837	Chatham Chest	

16 Pensions to Widows and Orphans contd

PRO References	Dates	Remarks	Series
Flag Officers, Captains, Commanders, Lieutenants, Masters, Surgeons, Pursers, Boatswains, Gunners, Carpenters			
ADM 6/222	1832-1835		
Flag Officers, Captains, Commanders, Lieutenants, Masters, Surgeons, Pursers, Boatswains, Gunners, Carpenters, Pilots			
ADM 22/50	1832-1835	Admiralty Pensions	
Flag Officers, Captains, Commanders, Lieutenants, Masters, Surgeons, Pursers, Boatswains, Gunners, Carpenters, Pilots			
ADM 23/29	1834-1837	Admiralty Pensions	
Flag Officers, Captains, Commanders, Lieutenants, Masters, Surgeons, Pursers, Boatswains, Gunners, Carpenters			
ADM 23/45-46	1836-1839		BA
Flag Officers, Captains, Commanders, Lieutenants, Masters, Surgeons, Pursers, Boatswains, Gunners, Carpenters			
PMG 16/2-5	1836-1847	Admiralty Pensions	AX
Flag Officers, Captains, Commanders, Lieutenants, Masters, Surgeons, Pursers, Engineers, Boatswains, Gunners, Carpenters, Chaplains			
ADM 23/55	1836-1863		
Flag Officers, Captains, Commanders, Lieutenants, Masters, Surgeons, Pursers ,Boatswains, Gunners, Carpenters			
PMG 19	1836-1929		AQ

16 Pensions to Widows and Orphans contd

	PRO References	Dates	Remarks	Series
Yard Officers	PMG 24	1836-1918	Admiralty Pensions	AY
Flag Officers, Captains, Commanders, Lieutenants, Masters, Surgeons, Pursers, Boatswains, Gunners, Carpenters, Chaplains	PMG 18	1837-1921	Compassionate List	AU
Flag Officers, Captains, Commanders, Lieutenants, Masters, Surgeons, Pursers, Boatswains, Gunners, Carpenters, Chaplains	ADM 23/106-107	1837-1878		
Engineers	PMG 18/7-38	1847-1921	Compassionate List	AU
Flag Officers, Captains, Commanders, Lieutenants, Masters, Surgeons, Pursers, Engineers, Boatswains, Gunners, Carpenters, Pilots	PMG 16/7-14	1848-1870	Admiralty Pensions	AX
Engineers	PMG 19/9-94	1849-1929	Admiralty Pensions	AQ
Engineers	PMG 16/7-14	1849-1870	Admiralty Pensions	AX
Flag Officers, Captains, Commanders, Lieutenants	ADM 23/95-100	1853-1901	Compassionate List	
Flag Officers, Captains, Commanders, Lieutenants, Masters, Surgeons, Pursers, Engineers, Boatswains, Gunners, Carpenters	ADM 23/76-77	1857-1876	Admiralty Pensions	
Coast Guard Officers & Ratings	ADM 23/17-21	1857-1884		EP
Coast Guard Officers & Ratings	PMG 23	1857-1935	Admiralty Pensions	AZ
Coast Guard Officers	PMG 19/15-94	1857-1929		AQ
Ratings	ADM 80/107	1863-1865	Accidental deaths	

16 Pensions to Widows and Orphans contd

	PRO References	Dates	Remarks	Series
Flag Officers, Captains, Commanders, Lieutenants, Masters, Surgeons, Pursers, Engineers, Boatswains, Gunners, Carpenters	ADM 23/30-31	1866-1880	Admiralty Pensions	BC
Flag Officers, Captains, Commanders, Lieutenants	ADM 23/42	1867-1870	Compassionate List	BB
Flag Officers, Captains, Commanders, Lieutenants, Masters, Surgeons, Pursers, Engineers, Boatswains, Gunners, Carpenters, Chaplains	ADM 23/47-52	1867-1880		BA
Flag Officers, Captains, Commanders, Lieutenants, Sub-Lieutenants, Masters, Surgeons, Pursers, Engineers, Boatswains, Gunners, Carpenters, Chaplains, Pilots	PMG 20/1-4	1870-1882	Admiralty Pensions	AX
Flag Officers, Captains, Commanders, Lieutenants	ADM 23/43-44	1873-1885	Compassionate List	BB
Flag Officers, Captains, Commanders, Lieutenants, Masters, Surgeons, Pursers, Engineers, Boatswains, Gunners, Carpenters, Chaplains, Coast Guard Officers	ADM 23/84-88	1880-1899	Admiralty Pensions	BC
Flag Officers, Captains, Commanders, Lieutenants, Masters, Surgeons, Pursers, Engineers, Boatswains, Gunners, Carpenters, Chaplains, Coast Guard Officers	ADM 23/108-123	1880-1899		BA

16 Pensions to Widows and Orphans contd

	PRO References	Dates	Remarks	Series
Boatswains, Gunners, Carpenters, Coast Guard, Ratings	ADM 162/1-2	1881-1911	GH Grants to orphan girls	
Flag Officers, Captains, Commanders, Lieutenants, Mates, Sub-Lieutenants, Masters, Surgeons, Pursers, Engineers ,Boatswains, Gunners, Carpenters, Chaplains, Pilots	PMG 20/6	1882-1885	Admiralty Pensions	AX
Ratings	ADM 166/1-11	1882-1917	GH Widows' Pensions	
Flag Officers, Captains, Commanders, Lieutenants	ADM 163	1883-1922	GH Education Grants	
Coast Guard Officers & Ratings	ADM 23/71-75	1884-1902		EP
Boatswains, Gunners, Carpenters, Coast Guard, Ratings	ADM 162/3-8	1884-1959	GH Grants to orphan boys	
Flag Officers, Captains, Commanders, Lieutenants, Mates, Sub-Lieutenants, Masters, Surgeons, Pursers, Engineers, Boatswains, Gunners, Carpenters, Chaplains, Pilots	PMG 20/8	1885-1888	Admiralty Pensions	AX
Boatswains, Gunners, Carpenters	PMG 18/21-38	1885-1921	Compassionate List	AU
Flag Officers, Captains, Commanders, Lieutenants, Mates, Sub-Lieutenants, Masters, Surgeons, Pursers, Engineers, Boatswains, Gunners, Carpenters, Chaplains, Pilots	PMG 20/10	1888-1891	Admiralty Pensions	AX
Schoolmasters	PMG 19/51-94	1889-1929		AQ
Schoolmasters	ADM 23/115-123	1889-1899		BA

16 Pensions to Widows and Orphans contd

	PRO References	Dates	Remarks	Series
Flag Officers, Captains, Commanders, Lieutenants, Sub-Lieutenants, Masters, Surgeons, Pursers, Engineers, Boatswains, Gunners, Carpenters, Chaplains, Pilots	PMG 20/12	1891-1895	Admiralty Pensions	AX
Ratings	ADM 166/13-14	1892-1933	GH Widows' Pensions, applications	
Flag Officers, Captains, Commanders, Lieutenants, Mates, Sub-Lieutenants, Masters, Surgeons, Pursers, Engineers, Boatswains, Gunners, Carpenters, Chaplains, Pilots	PMG 20/17-20	1895-1911	Admiralty Pensions	AX
Artificer Engineers	ADM 23/121-123	1897-1899		BA
Artificer Engineers	PMG 19/59-94	1897-1929		AQ
Flag Officers, Captains, Commanders, Lieutenants, Mates, Sub-Lieutenants, Masters, Surgeons, Pursers, Engineers, Boatswains, Gunners, Carpenters, Chaplains, Coast Guard Officers, Schoolmasters, Artificer Engineers	ADM 23/161-164	1899-1915	Admiralty Pensions	BC
Flag Officers, Captains, Commanders, Lieutenants, Mates, Sub-Lieutenants, Masters, Surgeons, Pursers, Engineers, Boatswains, Gunners, Carpenters, Chaplains, Coast Guard Officers, Schoolmasters, Artificer Engineers	ADM 23/145-160	1899-1932		BA

16 Pensions to Widows and Orphans contd

	PRO References	Dates	Remarks	Series
Wardmasters	ADM 23/161-164	1900-1915	Admiralty Pensions	BC
Wardmasters	PMG 19/63-94	1900-1929		AQ
Wardmasters	ADM 23/145-160	1900-1932		BA
Ratings	ADM 166/12	1901-1917	GH Widows' Pensions	
Flag Officers, Captains, Commanders, Lieutenants, Masters, Surgeons, Pursers, Engineers	ADM 23/200-205	1902-1926	Compassionate List	BB
Coast Guard Officers & Ratings	ADM 23/194-199	1902-1926		EP
Flag Officers, Captains, Commanders, Lieutenants	ADM 164	1907-1933	GH Education Grants	
Wt. Writers, Telegraphists, Stewards & Mechanicians	PMG 19/71-94	1910-1929		AQ
Flag Officers, Captains, Commanders, Lieutenants, Mates, Sub-Lieutenants, Masters, Surgeons, Pursers, Engineers, Boatswains, Gunners, Carpenters, Chaplains, Pilots	PMG 20/22-23	1911-1919	Admiralty Pensions	AX
Wt. Instructors in Cookery, Chief Masters at Arms, Artificer Engineers, Wt. Telegraphists, Electricians, Writers, Armourers, Ordnance Officers & Stewards	ADM 23/164	1911-1915	Admiralty Pensions	BC
Wt. Instructors in Cookery, Chief Masters at Arms, Artificer Engineers, Wt. Telegraphists, Electricians, Writers, Armourers, Ordnance Officers & Stewards	ADM 23/151-160	1911-1932		BA

16 Pensions to Widows and Orphans contd

	PRO References	Dates	Remarks	Series
Canteen Managers, RFA Officers	PMG 56	1914-1928	Admiralty Pensions	
Flag Officers, Captains, Commanders, Lieutenants, Mates, Sub-Lieutenants, Masters, Surgeons, Pursers, Engineers, Boatswains, Gunners, Carpenters, Chaplains, Coast Guard & other Wt. & Cd. Wt. Officers	ADM 23/168	1916-1918	Admiralty Pensions	BC
Flag Officers, Captains, Commanders, Lieutenants, Mates, Sub-Lieutenants, Masters, Surgeons, Pursers, Engineers, Boatswains, Gunners, Carpenters, Chaplains, Coast Guard & other Wt. & Cd. Wt. Officers	PMG 43/1	1916-1920	Supplementary	
Flag Officers, Captains, Commanders, Lieutenants, Mates, Sub-Lieutenants, Masters, Surgeons, Pursers, Engineers, Boatswains, Gunners, Carpenters, Chaplains, Coast Guard & other Wt. & Cd. Wt. Officers	PMG 44/8-9	1916-1920	Admiralty Pensions	
Flag Officers, Captains, Commanders, Lieutenants, Mates, Sub-Lieutenants, Masters, Surgeons, Pursers, Engineers, Boatswains, Gunners, Carpenters, Chaplains, Coast Guard & other Wt. & Cd. Wt. Officers	ADM 23/169	1921-1932	Admiralty Pensions	BC
Ratings	PMG 72/1-2	1921-1926	(new grants)	
RNR Ratings	ADM 23/170	1922-1925	Admiralty Pensions	

16 Pensions to Widows and Orphans contd

	PRO References	Dates	Remarks	Series
Boatswains, Gunners, Carpenters, Coast Guard, Ratings	ADM 162/9	1951-1959	GH Grants to orphan girls	

17 Other Pensions

	PRO References	Dates	Remarks	Series
Midshipmen, Masters, Pursers, Boatswains, Gunners, Carpenters, Chaplains, Cooks, Ratings	ADM 82/1-2	1653-1657	Chatham Chest	
Flag Officers, Captains, Commanders, Lieutenants	ADM 18/53-119	1673-1781	Wounds	AM
Midshipmen, Surgeons, Boatswains, Gunners, Carpenters, Cooks, Ratings	ADM 82/12-119	1675-1799	Chatham Chest	AN
Flag Officers, Captains, Commanders, Lieutenants, Masters, Surgeons	ADM 7/809-814	1689-1785	Wounds	AO
Flag Officers, Captains, Commanders, Lieutenants, Masters, Surgeons, Pursers	ADM 181/1-27	1708-1818	Wounds	EM
Ratings	ADM 82/122-123	1759-1794	Chatham Chest	
Lieutenants	ADM 22/1-5	1781-1793	Wounds	AM
Lieutenants	ADM 22/17-30	1793-1821	Wounds	AM
Captains, Commanders, Lieutenants	ADM 22/254	1814	GH Out-Pensions	BE
Midshipmen, Surgeons, Pursers, Boatswains, Gunners, Carpenters, Cooks, Yard Officers, Ratings	ADM 22/254-443	1814-1846	GH Out-Pensions	BD
Captains, Commanders, Lieutenants	ADM 22/47-49	1815-1842	GH Out-Pensions	BE
Flag Officers, Captains, Commanders, Lieutenants, Masters, Surgeons, Pursers	ADM 23/22-23	1830-1836	Wounds	

17 Other Pensions contd

	PRO References	Dates	Remarks	Series
Boatswains, Gunners, Carpenters, Cooks, Yard Officers, Artificers, Pilots, Ratings	ADM 22/52-55	1831-1837	Chatham Chest	
Flag Officers, Captains, Commanders, Lieutenants	ADM 6/222	1832-1835	Wounds	
Flag Officers, Captains, Commanders, Lieutenants	ADM 6/270	1835-1837	GH Out-Pension applicants	
Flag Officers, Captains, Commanders, Lieutenants, Masters, Surgeons, Pursers	PMG 16/1	1836-1838	Wounds	BF
Flag Officers, Captains	ADM 23/23	1837	Good Service Pensions	
Flag Officers, Captains, Commanders, Lieutenants, Cadets, Masters, Surgeons, Pursers	PMG 16/3-6	1839-1850	Wounds & Good Service Pensions	BF
Mates	PMG 16/3-6	1840-1850	Wounds	BF
Captains, Commanders, Lieutenants, Masters	PMG 71	1846-1921	GH Out-Pensions	BE
Engineers	PMG 16/6	1848-1850	Wounds	BF
Flag Officers, Captains	PMG 16/8-31	1851-1920	Wounds & Good Service Pensions	BF
Commanders, Lieutenants, Mates, Sub-Lieutenants, Midshipmen, Cadets, Masters, Surgeons, Pursers, Engineers	PMG 16/8-31	1851-1920	Wounds	BF

	PRO References	Dates	Remarks	Series
17 Other Pensions contd				
Flag Officers, Captains	ADM 23/76-77	1857-1876	Wounds & Good Service Pensions	
Commanders, Lieutenants, Mates, Sub-Lieutenants, Midshipmen, Cadets, Masters, Surgeons, Pursers, Engineers	ADM 23/76-77	1857-1876	Wounds	
Flag Officers, Captains	ADM 165	1865-1961	GH Pensions	
Flag Officers, Captains, Commanders, Lieutenants, Sub-Lieutenants, Midshipmen, Cadets, Masters, Surgeons, Pursers	ADM 23/32	1866-1869	Wounds	BH
Flag Officers, Captains, Commanders, Lieutenants, Masters, Surgeons, Pursers, Engineers, Boatswains, Gunners, Carpenters, Chaplains	PMG 70	1866-1928	GH Pensions	
Chaplains	ADM 6/446	1866-1909	Applicants for GH Out-Pensions	
Midshipmen, Cadets, Boatswains, Gunners, Carpenters	PMG 16/13-31	1867-1921	Wounds	BF
Flag Officers, Captains, Commanders, Sub-Lieutenants, Midshipmen, Cadets, Masters, Pursers	ADM 23/24	1870-1880	Wounds	
Flag Officers, Captains, Commanders, Lieutenants, Sub-Lieutenants, Midshipmen, Cadets, Masters, Surgeons, Pursers, Engineers, Boatswains, Gunners, Carpenters, Chaplains	ADM 23/89-94	1871-1900	Wounds	BH

17 Other Pensions contd

	PRO References	Dates	Remarks	Series
Commanders, Lieutenants, Masters, Surgeons, Pursers, Engineers, Boatswains, Gunners, Carpenters, Chaplains	ADM 165	1871-1961	GH Pensions	BG
Schoolmasters	PMG 16/23-31	1889-1920	Wounds	BF
Coast Guard Officers	ADM 23/93-94	1895-1900	Wounds	BF
Coast Guard Officers	PMG 16/24-31	1895-1920	Wounds	BF
Artificer Engineers	PMG 16/25-31	1897-1920	Wounds	BF
Wardmasters	PMG 16/26-31	1900-1920	Wounds	BF
Wt. Mechanicians, Telegraphists, Stewards & Writers	PMG 16/28-31	1910-1920	Wounds	BF
Wt. Armourers & Electricians	PMG 16/28-31	1911-1920	Wounds	BF
Flag Officers, Captains	ADM 23/206-207	1916-1928	Wounds & Good Service Pensions	BH
Commanders, Lieutenants, Mates, Sub-Lieutenants, Midshipmen, Cadets, Masters, Surgeons, Pursers, Engineers, Boatswains, Gunners, Carpenters, Chaplains, Coast Guard Officers	ADM 23/206-207	1916-1928	Wounds	BH
Flag Officers, Captains, Commanders, Lieutenants, Mates, Sub-Lieutenants, Midshipmen, Cadets, Surgeons, Pursers, Engineers, Boatswains, Gunners, Carpenters, Chaplains, Other Wt. & Cd. Wt. Officers	PMG 42/13-14	1917-1919	Wounds	

17 Other Pensions contd

	PRO References	Dates	Remarks	Series
Flag Officers, Captains	ADM 23/144	1928-1931	Wounds & Good Service Pensions	BH
Commanders, Lieutenants, Mates, Sub-Lieutenants, Midshipmen, Cadets, Masters, Surgeons, Pursers, Engineers, Boatswains, Gunners, Carpenters, Chaplains, Coast Guard Officers	ADM 23/144	1928-1931	Wounds	BH

18 Passing Certificates

	PRO References	Dates	Remarks	Series
Masters	SP 46/136-137	1660-1673	Trinity House	BI
Masters	ADM 106/2908-2950	1660-1830		BJ
Lieutenants	ADM 107/1-63	1691-1832	Home	BK
Surgeons	ADM 106/2952-2963	c1700-1800		BL
Gunners	ADM 6/123-124	1731-1748		BM
Lieutenants	ADM 6/86-88	1744-1780		
Pilots	ADM 30/36	1759-1770		
Gunners	ADM 6/125-127	1760-1797		BL
Lieutenants	ADM 6/89-116	1781-1819	Home	BM
Lieutenants	ADM 6/117-118	1788-1818	Abroad	
Lieutenants	ADM 1/5123/3	1794-1803	Abroad, Strays	
Lieutenants	ADM 107/64-70	1795-1832	Register	BN
Masters	ADM 6/135-168	c1800-1850		Q
Lieutenants	ADM 30/31	1801-1810	Failing Certificates	
Gunners	ADM 6/128-129	1803-1812		BL

18 Passing Certificates contd

	PRO References	Dates	Remarks	Series
Boatswains	ADM 6/122	1810–1813		
Pursers	ADM 6/120	1813–1820		
Lieutenants, Mates, Sub-Lieutenants	ADM 11/22	1829–1865	Register	
Masters	ADM 13/72–74	1851–1863		BS
Pursers	ADM 13/79–82	1851–1867		
Boatswains	ADM 13/83	1851–1855		
Carpenters	ADM 13/83–84	1851–1860		
Clerks	ADM 13/75–78	1852–1867		
Naval Instructors	ADM 13/246	1853–1872		
Seaman Schoolmasters	ADM 13/246	1853–1866		
Lieutenants	ADM 13/88–101	1854–1867		BP
Clerks	ADM 13/196–199	1856–1899		
Boatswains	ADM 13/85	1856–1859		
Gunners	ADM 13/86–87	1856–1863		
Midshipmen	ADM 13/102	1857–1866		BR
Boatswains	ADM 13/193–194	1860–1887		
Carpenters	ADM 13/195	1861–1887		
Engineers	ADM 13/200–205	1863–1902		BQ
Gunners	ADM 13/249–250	1864–1887		
Lieutenants, Mates, Sub-Lieutenants	ADM 11/89	1865–1880	Register	
Midshipmen	ADM 13/240–245	1867–1899		BR
Lieutenants	ADM 13/207–236	1868–1902		BP
Pursers	ADM 13/247–248	1868–1889		BS
Lieutenants	ADM 13/238	1869–1885	In Navigation	
Lieutenants	ADM 13/237	1869–1882	In Gunnery	

	PRO References	Dates	Remarks	Series
18 Passing Certificates contd				
Engine Room Artificers	ADM 13/206	1877-1886		
Lieutenants	ADM 13/251	1895-1897	From Acting Sub-Lieutenant	
19 Full Pay				
Surgeons	ADM 20/1-72	1660-1672	Various Payments	BT
All Officers & Ratings	SP 46/138	1661-1663	Arrears	
Yard Officers, Pilots	ADM 18/39-119	1666-1781		AM
Surgeons	ADM 82/3-11	1681-1743	Twopences	BU
Chaplains	ADM 82/3-11	1681-1743	Ministers' Groats	BU
Yard Officers	ADM 7/809-821	1689-1832	Only Foreign and Minor Yards from 1708	AO
Surgeons, Nurses	ADM 102/863	1742	Jamaica Hospital	
Surgeons, Nurses	ADM 102/375-397	1769-1819	Haslar Hospital	
Surgeons, Nurses	ADM 102/683-700	1777-1819	Plymouth Hospital	
Yard Officers	ADM 22/1-16	1781-1819		AM
Surgeons	ADM 102/851-852	1789-1803	'Free Gifts'	
Pilots	ADM 30/37-39	1793-1807	Claims for Pilotage	
Flag Officers	ADM 24/1	1795-1817		BV
Captains, Commanders	ADM 24/2-11	1795-1817		BV
Lieutenants	ADM 24/12-38	1795-1817		BV
Masters	ADM 24/40-50	1795-1817		BV
Surgeons	ADM 24/51-65	1795-1817		BV
Boatswains, Gunners, Carpenters, Ratings	ADM 27	1795-1852	Allotments	BW

19 Full Pay contd

	PRO References	Dates	Remarks	Series
Chaplains	ADM 24/66-67	1795-1817		BV
Ratings	ADM 26	1795-1851	Remittances	BX-BZ
Surgeons, Nurses	ADM 102	1796ff	Pay Lists of hospitals and hospital ships	
Ratings	ADM 28	1798-1810	Sea Fencibles	
Captains, Commanders	ADM 24/85-88	1804-1820		BV
Mates, Sub-Lieutenants	ADM 24/39	1805-1814		BV
Chaplains	ADM 30/7	1805-1822	Chaplains' Bounty	
Yard Officers	ADM 7/859	1808-1823	Home Yards	
Chaplains	ADM 24/83	1811-1818		BV
Midshipmen, 2nd Masters, Clerks	ADM 24/89	1817-1820		
Surgeons	ADM 105/1-9	1817-1832	Decisions & precedents	BV
Lieutenants	ADM 24/69-76	1818-1830		BV
Surgeons	ADM 24/77-82	1818-1830		BV
Ship's Company	ADM 30/63/18	1821-1822	HMS *Bathurst*	
Surgeons	ADM 105/10-19	1822-1832	Decisions & precedents	
Yard Officers	ADM 7/861	1822-1832	Home Yards	
Flag Officers, Captains, Commanders, Lieutenants, Mates, Sub-Lieutenants, Midshipmen, Cadets, Masters, Surgeons, Pursers, Chaplains, Coast Guard Officers	ADM 24/93-170	1830-1872		BV

19 Full Pay contd

	PRO References	Dates	Remarks	Series
Engineers	ADM 22/444-449	1847-1858		CA
Boatswains	ADM 22/458-460	1853-1858		CB
Carpenters	ADM 22/465-468	1853-1872		CC
Gunners	ADM 22/469-474	1854-1872		CD
Engineers	ADM 22/450-457	1858-1873		CA
Boatswains	ADM 22/461-464	1858-1874		CB
Engineers	ADM 29/113	1871-1873		CA

20 Superannuation & Retirement Pensions

	PRO References	Dates	Remarks	Series
Captains	ADM 18/39-97	1666-1747		AM
Yard Officers	ADM 18/39-119	1666-1781		AM
Masters, Surgeons, Pursers, Boatswains, Gunners, Carpenters, Cooks	ADM 18/50-119	1672-1781		AM
Captains	ADM 7/809-812	1689-1747		AO
Flag Officers, Masters, Surgeons, Pursers, Boatswains, Gunners, Carpenters, Cooks, Yard Officers, Pilots	ADM 7/809-814	1689-1785		AO
Ratings	ADM 73/51-62	1704-1863	GH In-Pensions	CF
Ratings	ADM 73/36-41	1704-1846	GH In-Pensions	CE
Masters, Surgeons, Pursers, Boatswains, Gunners, Carpenters, Cooks, Pilots, Yard Officers	ADM 181/1-18	1708-1811		EM

20 Superannuation & Retirement Pensions contd

	PRO References	Dates	Remarks	Series
Lieutenants	ADM 18/92-119	1737-1781		AM
Lieutenants	ADM 7/811-814	1737-1785		AO
Ratings	ADM 6/223-266	1737-1859	Candidates for GH	CG
Lieutenants	ADM 181/3-18	1737-1811		EM
Flag Officers ('Yellow Admirals')	ADM 181/4-18	1747-1811		EM
Flag Officers ('Yellow Admirals')	ADM 18/98-119	1747-1781		AM
Ratings	ADM 73/65-69	1764-1865	GH In-Pensions	CI
Ratings	ADM 73/42-50	1779-1866	GH In-Pensions	CH
Flag Officers, Captains, Commanders, Lieutenants, Masters, Surgeons, Pursers, Boatswains, Gunners, Carpenters, Cooks, Pilots	ADM 22/1-5	1781-1793		AM
Yard Officers	ADM 22/1-16	1781-1819		AM
Ratings	ADM 73/95-131	1781-1809	GH Out-Pensions	CJ
Captains	ADM 181/9-18	1786-1811		EM
Ratings	ADM 6/271-322	1789-1859	Candidates for GH	CK
Ratings	ADM 73/1-35	1790-1865	GH In-Pensions	P
Flag Officers, Captains Commanders, Lieutenants, Masters, Surgeons, Pursers, Boatswains, Gunners, Carpenters, Cooks, Pilots	ADM 22/17-30	1793-1821		AM
French Pilots	ADM 30/40	1802-1809		
Flag Officers, Captains, Commanders, Lieutenants, Masters, Surgeons, Pursers, Boatswains, Gunners, Carpenters, Cooks, Yard Officers, Pilots				

20 Superannuation & Retirement Pensions contd

	PRO References	Dates	Remarks	Series
Ratings	ADM 6/267-269	1813-1834	Candidates for GH	BD
Ratings	ADM 22/254-443	1814-1846	GH Out Pensions	AV
Flag Officers, Captains, Commanders, Lieutenants, Masters, Surgeons, Pursers, Boatswains, Gunners, Carpenters, Cooks, Yard Officers, Pilots	ADM 22/31-36	1818-1826		
Flag Officers, Captains, Commanders, Lieutenants, Masters, Boatswains, Gunners, Carpenters, Cooks, Pilots	ADM 22/39-46	1828-1831	Outports	AW
Boatswains, Gunners, Carpenters, Cooks, Coast Guard	ADM 23/22-23	1830-1836		
Nurses	ADM 23/1-16	1830-1884		BO
Flag Officers, Captains, Commanders, Lieutenants, Masters, Surgeons, Pursers, Boatswains, Gunners, Carpenters, Cooks, Yard Officers, Pilots	ADM 22/50	1832-1834		
Boatswains, Gunners, Carpenters, Cooks	ADM 6/222	1832-1835		
Yard Officers, Hospital Matrons	ADM 23/25	1834-1836		EQ
Flag Officers, Captains, Commanders, Lieutenants, Masters, Surgeons, Pursers, Chaplains	PMG 15/1-3	1836-1838		CL
Boatswains, Gunners, Carpenters, Cooks	PMG 16/1	1836-1838		CM

20 *Superannuation & Retirement Pensions contd*

	PRO References	Dates	Remarks	Series
Yard Officers, Hospital Matrons	PMG 24	1836-1918		AY
Pilots	PMG 16/2-5	1836-1847		AX
Nurses	PMG 25	1836-1928		CN
Flag Officers, Captains, Commanders	PMG 15/5	1838-1840		CL
Lieutenants, Chaplains	PMG 15/6	1838-1840		CL
Masters, Surgeons, Pursers	PMG 15/7	1838-1840		CL
Boatswains, Gunners, Carpenters, Cooks	PMG 16/3-6	1839-1850		CM
Flag Officers, Captains, Commanders, Lieutenants, Mates, Masters, Surgeons, Pursers, Chaplains	PMG 15/9-13	1840-1843		CL
Surgeons	ADM 104/66	c1840	(Compiled) Inc. Physicians	
Ratings	WO 22	1842-1862	GH Out-Pensions	ER
Flag Officers, Captains, Commanders, Lieutenants, Mates, Masters, Surgeons, Pursers, Chaplains	PMG 15/15-19	1843-1846		CL
Flag Officers, Captains, Commanders, Lieutenants, Mates, Masters, Surgeons, Pursers, Chaplains	PMG 15/21-25	1846-1849		CL
Engineers	PMG 16/6	1847-1850		CM
Pilots	PMG 16/7-14	1848-1870		AX
Flag Officers, Captains, Commanders, Lieutenants, Mates, Sub-Lieutenants, Masters, Surgeons, Pursers, Chaplains	PMG 16/27-73	1849-1876		CL
Flag Officers	PMG 16/8-25	1851-1900		BF

20 *Superannuation & Retirement Pensions contd*

	PRO References	Dates	Remarks	Series
Engineers, Boatswains, Gunners, Carpenters, Cooks	PMG 16/8-17	1851-1874		CM
Inspectors of Machinery & Chief Engineers	PMG 15/32-73	1853-1876		CL
Yard Officers	ADM 23/76-77	1857-1876		AZ
Coast Guard	PMG 23	1857-1935		
Coast Guard	ADM 23/17-21	1857-1884		EP
Ratings	ADM 73/63-64	1863-1869	GH In- and Out-Pensions	
Engineers, Boatswains, Gunners, Carpenters, Cooks	ADM 23/32	1866-1869	Engineers & Asst. Engineers only	
Yard Officers, Hospital Matrons	ADM 23/26-28	1866-1884		EQ
Flag Officers, Captains, Commanders, Lieutenants, Masters, Surgeons, Pursers	ADM 23/33-34	1867-1871		CP
Engineers, Boatswains, Gunners, Carpenters, Chaplains	ADM 23/33-34	1867-1871	Engineers & Asst. Engineers only	CO
Ratings	WO 23/24	1868-1870	Ex-GH In-Pensions	
Engineers, Boatswains, Gunners, Carpenters, Cooks, Coast Guard Wt. Officers	ADM 23/24	1870-1880	Engineers & Asst. Engineers only (granted to 1877)	
Pilots	PMG 20/1-4	1870-1882		AX
Flag Officers, Captains, Commanders, Lieutenants, Masters, Surgeons, Pursers	ADM 23/36-41	1871-1881		CP

Commissions dated 31. August 1739 for

Mr John Morris to be — 3d — Deptford
Mr Tobias Pye — 4. Prince of Orange
Mr Nicholas Cooper — Salamander Bomb
Mr Robert Baynes — Tryal Sloop
Mr Robert Wilson — Cumberland Fireship
Mr Peregrine Bradshaw — 4 — Grafton
Mr Step. Pollington — 3. Warwick
Hon.ble Mr John Bermingham — 3 Panther
Mr Jervas Henry Porter — 4. Pr. Amelia
Mr Francis Arundel — 4. Norfolk
Mr George Ryal — 3. York
Lieut Jonathan Russel — 3. Rippon
Mr Molyneux Shuldham — 3. Tilbury
Mr Richard Lee — 3. Defyance
Mr John Brown — 3. Litchfield
Mr George Langdon — 3. Winchester
Mr Richard Davies — 3. Bristol
Mr John Legge — 3. Rochester
Mr William Walton — 3. Ludlow Castle

C Wager T Frankland T Clutterbuck

By &c

J Burchett

Warrant dated 3 September 1739 for
John Pridgeon to be Master at Arms of the
Sunderland
C W. T F. T C.

Commission dated 1. Septr 1739 for
Plyr. Lieut. George Cockburne to be 3d. Litchfield
C W. T F. T C. J C.

Figure 1   Entries in the Commission and Warrant Book of 1735-1742 (ADM 6/15)

In pursuance of the directions of the Rt Honble the Lords Comm: of the Admiralty, signified to Us by Mr Corbetts Letter of the 14 August 1744, Wee have examin'd Mr Justinian Nutt, who by Certificate appears to be more than Forty years of Age, and find he has gone to Sea more than Thirteen years in the Ships and Qualitys undermentiond Viz:

Ships	Quality	Time ye ms ws ds
Biddeford	Lievt Servt	2 : 8 : 2 : 3
Do	Able	3 : 3 : 3 : 1
Do	Corporal	1 : 4 : 1 : 1
York	Mars Mate	1 : 11 : 3 : 2
Centurion	Mar	3 : 0 : 1 : 4
Centurions prize	5th Lievt	0 : 3 : 2 : 4
Centurion	3d Lievt	0 : 10 : 1 : 1
		13 : 3 : 3 : 2

He produceth Journals kept by him in the York & Centurion, and Certificates from Capt Anson & Capt Saumarez, of his diligence, Sobriety and obedience to Command. he can Splice, Knott, Reef a Sail, Work a Ship in Sailing, Shift his Tides, keep a Reckoning of a Ships Way, by plain Sailing & Mercator, Observe by Sun or Star, find the Variation of the Compass, and is qualified to do the duty of an able Seaman & Midshipman. Dated at the Navy Office the 31 August 1744

Figure 2 Passing Certificate of Lieutenant Justinian Nutt, 1744 (ADM 6/86)

Comet Galley Complement 40 Men & Order Began Wages &c. the 11th Octr 1780 & Ended the 16th July 1782
of Capt. William Bell, 11 Octer 1780. Charlestown So Carolina

Bounty Paid	No	Entry	Year	Appearance	Whence and Whether Prest or not.	Place and County where Born	Age at Time of Entry in this Ship	No and Letter of Tickets	MENS NAMES	Quality	D.D.D. or R.	Time of Discharge	Year	Whither or for what Reason	Stragling	Front of Ledger	Marine Deductions	
																	Necessaries	Stopages
	1	Octr 1780	Octr 11						John Saunders	Ab	D	Jan 1782						
									Law. Kelly		D	No 6 1780						
				Of Commission Octr 11 1780					And. Law		D	July 1 1782						
					Kingsley Antigua	22		John Dutie		R	Feb 12		Charleston				
5		12		12	Prest Port Glasgow	21		Dan. Todd	Ab	R	Jan 18 1781		Do				
		13		13	Vol Charlestown Carolina	19		Isaac Harvey		R	Nov 20		Capefair				
		15		15	Prest Marseilles	22		John Vincent	Ab	R	July 22		Do				
				Vol Dublin	26		George Gibson	Ab	R	Jan 10		Charleston				
		16		16	Isle Providence	20		Dan. Baker	Ab	R	Aug 20		Capefair				
10		20		20	Dundee	43		Dav. Grigg		D	July 16 1782						
		31		31	Vol Middlesex	32		James Denton		R	April 22						
				East Riding	27		John Boulder	Ab	R	Nov 28 1781		Capefair				
	No 1		No 1	Prest Cork	32		Hercules Ronney	Ab	R	Jan 18		Charleston				
				Isle Providence	28		John Johnson	Ab	R	Aug 20		Capefair				
15		2		2	Vol Charlestown Carolina	28		Sam. Long	Ab	D	Jan 17						
		7		7	Savannah Georgia	34		David Davis	Ab	R	June 24 1782		Ashley River				
				St Augustine	23		Samuel Small	Ab	D			Do				
18		12		12	Prest Isle Jersey	24		Claud Bignx	Ab	R	Nov 15 1781		Capefair				

1

Figure 3   Pay Book of *Comet* Galley, 1780-1782 (ADM 30/45)

In the Name of God, I Joseph Lewis Able Seaman late belonging to His Majesty's Ship Leander, but now to His Majesty's Sloop Bull Dog (No 190 on the Ships Books) in the New Mole of Gibraltar, being of sound and disposing Mind and Memory, do hereby make this my last Will and Testament, First and Principally I commend my Soul into the Hands of Almighty God, hoping for Remission of all my Sins through the Merits of Jesus Christ my Blessed Saviour and Redeemer, and my Body to the Earth or Sea as it shall please God, And as for such Worldly Estate and Effects, which I shall be possessed of, or entitled unto at the time of my Decease; I give and bequeath unto my trusty Friend Thomas Peyton Esquire Commander of His Majesty's said Sloop Bull Dog, all such Wages, Sum, and Sums of Money as now is due to me from His Majesty's Ship Leander, as also whatever is now, or hereafter shall be due for my Service or otherwise on board the said Sloop Bull Dog, or any Ship or Vessel, And I do hereby nominate, constitute and appoint my said trusty Friend Thomas Peyton Esquire, Executor of this my last Will and Testament, hereby revoking and making Void, all other and former Wills by me heretofore made, And do declare this to be my last Will and Testament, In Witness whereof I have hereunto set my Hand and Seal this twenty seventh day of October in the Year of our Lord one Thousand, seven Hundred & Ninety, & in the Thirty First Year of the Reign of our Sovereign Lord George the Third by the Grace of God, of Great Britain, France, and Ireland, King Defender of the Faith &c².

Signed, Sealed, Published and declared
by the said Joseph Lewis, as and for his last
Will and Testament in the Presence of us, who
have hereunto subscribed our Names, as Witnesses
in the Presence of the said Testat. —

Joseph Lewis

Tho. Peyton ⎰ Pickett, Master
Captain ⎱ W. Crisp, Purser

Figure 4 Will of Able Seaman Joseph Lewis, 1790 (ADM 48/53)

Captain Henry Prescott, CB,

Entered the Service,	16 Feb. 1796,
Lieutenant,	28 April 1802,
Commander,	4 Feb 1808,
Captain,	25 July 1810,

Was Midshipman of the Penelope at the capture of the mound Tell, a French 80 gun ship, in March 1800; — Was Lieutenant of the Rolus in Sir Richard Strachan's action of 4 Novr 1805; — In 1808, when in command of the Weazle, 18 guns, assisted at the capture of four large gun-boats, and thirty-four coasting vessels; — in October 1809, captured le Veloce French letter of Marque of 4 guns, and, in December following l'Eole of 14 guns, after a gallant resistance of an hour and a half; — in 1810, being still in the Weazle, made several prizes and recaptures; was repeatedly engaged with the enemy's flotilla, and assisted in the capture and destruction of a large convoy from Naples; — The same year particularly distinguished himself at Amanthea, where he commanding the landing-party consisting of seamen and Marines, and after capturing six gun-vessels, brought off a gun, under a heavy fire of musketry; — Captain Prescott was promoted for this service; —

Has been actively employed afloat as a commissioned officer, nearly fifteen years.

Figure 5   Statement of Service for Captain Harry Prescott, CB, 1796-1810 (ADM 11/1)

Ruby 64 Guns 3 Rate

Date of Wt.	Names	Quality	Last ship they served in	Quality in last ship	Present Qualification	Where sent
10 May 99	Dav.d Wallace	Master	Colossus	Master	3.d Rate	Party
9 Jan.y 1800	Tho.s Stokes	Acting Do	Danæ	Master	5.th	Lyme
15 Apl 1801	Swan Blyth	Act.g Master	Babet	Master	5.th	Park
5 Aug 1801	Tho.s Robinson	Sailm.r	Majestic	Sailm.r		Capt.n o.n
10 Oct 1804	Wm Thomson	do first Appointment				Party
6 June 1803	R.d West	Master	Agamemnon	Master	3.d	
13 Nov.r 1805	Tho.s Fairlanger	Do	Aigle	Do	3.d	
27 May 1806	Peter Smith	Sailm.r	This			
13 Dec.r "	Fred.k Boxwell	Do				Sheerness
8 June 1807	John Lamb (2)	Master acting	Malabar	Master	5.t	

Romney 50 Guns 4 Rate

16 July 99	James Patterson	Caulker	first appointment			Sheerness
19 April 1800	James Downie	Acting Master	Lynx	Master	6.th	Sheerness
7 May "	Wm Watson	Caulker	America	Caul.r		Capt.t o.n
17 Nov.r 1800	Ja.s Downie	to continue Master	see his Papers	6.		
31 Oct 1804	Wm Kirby	Master	Calcutta	Master	3.rd	
14 Sept "	Wm Karr	Sailm.r	first appointment			Party
21 Oct "	Jn.o Cunningham	Sail.r	Do			Do
25 "	Wm Gibson	Caulker	Do			Do

Figure 6 Succession Book of 1799 showing non-standing warrant officers aboard HMS *Ruby* and HMS *Romney* (ADM 106/2901)

No. D/3165.

Name of the Seaman or Marine, _John Dawson : Prince of Wales_

Name and Address of the Claimant, _Mary Alton alias Dawson, sister, 17 New-street, Dublin_

	Sent.	Returned.
Forwarded Blank Petition to Minister of Claimant's Parish · · · · · · · · · ·		29 Aug 17
Search sent for to the Navy-Office · · · · · · · · · · · · · · · · · ·	1 Sep 17	10 Oct 17
Wrote to Sick and Wounded Department, Transport-Office · · · · · · · ·		
Wrote to Prisoners of War Department, Transport-Office · · · · · · · · · ·		
Wrote to the Out-Port to know if Wages have been paid		
Wrote Marine Head Quarters · · · · · · · · · · · · · ·		
Wrote to Greenwich Hospital ·		
Wrote to the Claimant _claim preceding the word save·_		

hear from the office also   2 Oct 17

No 7 to Min —   24 Oct 17

No 8 to Cashier   17 Dec 17

2y d 26th to Mr Baxter —   2 Feb 1818

Check approved No 3150

CLAIM _admitted 2 Oct 17_

CHECK or CERTIFICATE.

wrote 9 Dec 17. D Common

Figure 7 Seamen's Effects Papers for John Dawson, 1818 (ADM 44/D13)

Complement 23. *House Laborers.* vide for Boats 102.

1/. a day wages — Admiralty Order 23 April 1858 —

These Situations abolished by A.O. Nov 1863 —

Date of Appointment.	Name.	Date of Death, Discharge, or Resignation.	Vice.
	Richard Rowe	D. 19th May 1858	
	Stephen Smith	D. to Insp. 1 Jan 1863	
	Joseph Reed	D. 8. Febr 1860	
	Thomas Cartman	D. 12 June 1858	
	John Lane	D. 5 Sept 1860	
	James Brewer	D. 14 May 1862	To Long Leave
	William Hodge	D. 10 June 1858	
	Thomas Nicholls	D. 21 Decr 1859	
	Thomas Benson	D. 25 Jan 1860	
	Joseph Townsend	D. 30 Nov 1863 —	
	William Holliday	D.C.P. 22 June 1859	
	Thomas Hand	D. 28 April 1858	
	David Mahoney	D. 24 Sept 1858	
	George Veary	D. 30 Nov 1863	
	Thomas Wilkinson	D. 9 July 1858	
	Richard Smith	D. 4 July 1860	
	John Higgs	D. 1 May 1858	
	John Grant	D. 28 April 1868	
	Richard Brown	D. Insp. 22 Aug 1861	
1858 14 January	William Doil	D. 1 May 1858	
16 "	Joseph Courtnall	D. 14 Sept 1859	
4 February	Cornelius Chadwick	D. 22 July 1859	To be Shovelman
4 March	Richard Cockcroft	D. 26th Mar 1858	
27 "	James Brooks	D. 7 April "	
8 April	Richard Cockcroft	D. 30 March 1859	
29 "	Henry Stevens	D. 12 May 1858	
	John Taylor		
2 May	John West	D. 23 Oct 1858	
" "	John Cooke	D. 9 April 1859	
13 "	Charles Porch	Res. 23 June 1858	
20 "	William Henry Course	D. 2 Sept 1859	Richd Rowe
10 June	Charles McCann —	D. 8 Sept 1858	Hodge
12 "	Jeremiah Lynch	D. 23 June 1858	Cartman
24 "	Thos. Cartman	D. 4 Decr 1858	Lynch
" "	James Burkitt	D 24 Aug 1858	Porch
10 July	William Wood	D. 11 Aug 1858	Wilkinson
12 August	Thomas Wilkinson	D. Insp 15 Febr 1859	Wood
25 "	William Wood	D. 1 Sept 1858	Burkitt
2 Septr	James Burkitt	D. 22 Jan 1859	Wood
9 "	Moses Rushmarsh	D. 23 July 1860	McCann
25 "	Henry Poole	D. 20 Oct 1858	Mahoney
21 Oct.	David Mahoney	D. absent 24 Oct 1858	Poole
23 "	Henry Poole	Res. 17 Nov 1858	West
25 "	Frederick Powell	D. 20 March 1859	Mahoney
18 Nov.	Samuel Love	D. 30 Nov 1863	Poole
4 Decr	Neil McLean	D. 8 Decr 1858	Cartman
9 "	Thomas Cartman	D. Insp 28 Nov 1862	McLean
22 Jan 1859	Thomas Lasher	D. 24 Augt 1859	Burkitt

Figure 8   Register of House Labourers at Greenwich Hospital, 1847-1865 (ADM 73/86)

500

Officer's Name   Callaghan Charles

Last Ship and Rating before Promotion, H.M.S.   "Pelican" P.O. 1st Class.

Ship	Rank	Period of Service		Time served				REMARKS.
				In Commission		In Ordinary or Reserve		
		From	To	Years of 365 Days	Days	Years of 365 Days	Days	
from C.S. No 57813	Seaman Petty Officer		23 Dec 79	—	11	42		Boatswain 24 December 1879
Pelican sup	Boatsw	24 Dec 79	7 Feb 80					
Shannon	"	8 Feb 80	17 June 81					
Indus "	"	18 June 81	8 May 82					
Revenge	"	9 May 82	8 May 85					
Indus	"	9 May 85	3 June 85					
Leander	"	4 June 85	4 Apl 89					
Indus	"	5 Apl 89	31 Aug 89					
Indus	"	1 Sept 89	3 Feb 90	15	78			
Triumph	"	4 Feb 90	21 July 90					Pensioned 8 mch 95
Do Manoeuvres	"	22 July 90	27 Aug 90					
Do	"	28 Aug 90	3 May 91					11 mch 95
Do	"	4 May 91	3 Feb 93					
Vivid (2)	"	4 Feb 93	24 Mar 93					
Victory	"	25 Mar 93	13 July 94					
Trafalgar	"	14 July 94	15 Feb 95					
Vivid (2)	"	16 Feb 95	7 March 95					
Pension £95 a year		8 mch 95	31 March 30	26	120			
		1st April 30	30 June					
		1 July	25 Apl 39 Died per P.60					

Figure 9   Record of Service for Petty Officer 1st Class Charles Callaghan (ADM 196/31)

Mr. J. G. Stewart. MD.

Age 57.   57 in 1862

Entered Service   5 April 1825.   Deputy Inspector Genl 20 Oct 1845

Inspector General. 25 June 1861.

Ships	Rating	Dates of Appointments.	Discharges.	Remarks.
Eclair	Asst. Surgeon	Octr 1845.	Novr 1845.	Served as Asst. 4.4 In Victory Supt Harlequin, Serapis, Magnificent Pylades, Lord Suffield, Hyperion, Gloucester, Fernando Po, Surveying Party Fernando Po. Surveying Party, acting Surgeon.
Vindictive	5 April 1825	July 1847.	Aug 1847.	
Jamaica Hospl		Aug 1847.	July 1849.	
Malta Hospital	Surgeon	Mar 1851.	Aug 1855.	Served as Surgeon, 12.8 Fernando Po. Surveying Party, Deal Hospital, Pelorus, Pylades, Leveret, Garrison of Ascension, Andromache, Nautilus C.S. Egyptian C.S. British Sovereign Co Alfred, & Eclair.
Greenwich Hospl	14 Sept 1829	Aug 1855		
Plymouth Hospl		June 1861. I.G.		
	Deputy Inspector General. 20 Oct 1845.			__Assist. Surgeon.__ In 1829. whilst serving with Marines at Fernando Po. when Malignant Fever prevailed was the only Survivor out of 11 Medical Officers on shore and attached to Ships at that place.
	Will be superseded on 26. June / 62			__Surgeon.__ 20 October 1836 Capt W. Bate Commandant Ascension. Expressed in Public Orders his approbation of his conduct
	Promoted to be Inspector General of Plymouth Hospl. 25 June 1861 See other leaf & Continued page 11			25th September 1838. Sir John Franklin Praised him for his superior manner in which he superintended the Nautilus, Convict Ship with Females on board.

14 September 1840. Sir Wm Burnett Director General, gave him a certificate of being a zealous & efficient Medical Officer.

1845. Adml Purvis, late Comr Brazils. Certified to his skill and conduct whilst serving in Alfred; as Flag Surgeon from Novr 1841. to Aug 1845.

Volunteered and was appointed to Eclair, with Yellow fever on board

Carried forward.

Continued page 11

Figure 10   Record of Service for Dr J G Stewart, MD, Inspector General of Hospitals (ADM 105/75)

No. 197.

Continuous Service Engagement.

H.M.S. *Doris* Granada
9th September 186*7*.

When Men or Boys enter for Continuous and General Service, (*C.S.*) Commanding Officers are immediately to fill up this Form and to transmit it to the Accountant-General of the Navy, at the end of the Month, with the List of Engagements executed. (Form, No. 41, *vide* Paymaster's Instructions, Page 40, Article 120, Clause 7.)

Christian and Surname in full .... *James Lyne.*

Where Born.—[If born out of Her Majesty's Dominions, it must be stated whether the parents are British Subjects; Foreigners not being allowed to volunteer for Continuous Service.] *Liskeard. Cornwall.*

Date of Birth.—[Great care is to be taken that the date is correctly stated : and a careful examination is to be made of the written Documents produced by Boys in support of their alleged age, in order to ascertain that they have not been tampered with. *Vide*, Foot Note, Chap. IX, Art. 2, Page 78, Admiralty Instructions.] *1st April* 18*29*.

Description .... Height *5 ft 7½ in* Complexion *Fair*

Hair *Lt brown* Eyes *Blue*

Marks *none*

Ship in which he Volunteers .... *"Doris" List 5-No. 59* } and No. on Ship's Books

Date of Entry in Do. .... *8th February* 18*66*.

Rating in Do. .... *Leading Stoker*.

Date of *actually* Volunteering for Continuous Service .... } *7th September* 18*67*.

Commencement of Engagement .... *7th September* 18*67*.

Period of ditto .... *To complete time for pension*

No. on Ship's Books	Ship's name	Rate	Entry	Discharge	
79	Buzzard	Stoker	1 May 1857	30 Oct 1857	
79	do	do	1 May 1857	1 July 1857	
56	Valorous	Ldg Stoker	1 Sept 1857	8 July 1858	
56	do	do	9 July 1858	14 Aug 1861	
597	Indus	do	15 Aug 1861	21 Dec 61	
597	do	do	1 Jan 62	3 Inch 62	
50	Styx	do	4 Inch 62	31 Inch 63	
50	do	do	1 Ap. 63	31 Inch 64	
50	do	do	1 Ap. 64	25 Oct 1865	
14K 1109	Indus	do	26 Oct 65	7 Feb 66	
6	do	do	8 Feb 66	31 Dec 66	

Statement of all former Service in the Navy, whether as Seaman or Boy, with names of Ships and dates of Entry and Discharge; and when Men also served in Dockyards, Coastguard, or Revenue Vessels, the names of the Dockyards, Coastguard Stations, and Revenue Vessels, with period of Service, to be stated. If belonging to any Naval Reserve Force, state particulars ....

Late C.S. No. *38584*

If the Man has ever previously been entered for "C.S." the particulars of his former Engagement should be inserted here in Red Ink } *Ten* years, from *7th September* 18*57*.

[*See over.*]

65970

Names in full	Date of Birth 8 March 1842.
John Payne	Place of Birth Piddletrenthide Dorset

Date and Period of C.S. Engagement.	Personal Description.					Trade.	Gunnery Engagements
	Height.	Hair.	Eyes.	Complexion.	Wounds, Scars, or Marks.		
1 Oct. 1867. 10 years. 3589 b January 1879 to complete *Traced*	5.8	Brown	Hazel	Fair	None	Stoker	

Ships served in. Coast Guard. Seamen Riggers.	Ships' Books.		Rating, &c	G.C. Badges worn.	Period of Service.		Time.		Character.	If Discharged. Whither and for what cause.	Remarks.
	List.	No.			From	To	Years.	Days.			
Immortalité	5	245	Ly Stoker	1	14 Oct 7.	14 Mar 73			V. Good	Payne Hough	P.E. 1866
Indus	15	417	Ly Stok		15 Mch 73	18 Mch 73			V.G.	Asia	
Asia	15a	375	"		19 "	26 "			V.G.		
Argus	5	89	"		27 Mar	8 May 74					
D. of Wellington	15ª	1016	"		9 May 74	18 May "			Time only		
Asia	15ª	1240	"		19 May	31 Aug 74			V.G.		
Vigilant	5	26	"		1 Sept "	9 Oct "					
Indus	15ª	1362	"		10 Oct 74	21 Oct 74			V.G.		
Himalaya	5	123	"		22 Oct 74	14 May 75			Exemplary		
D. of Wellington	15ª	1857	"		15 May 75				V. Good		
Lynx	5	44	Cook 1.C		23 June 75	24 June 75					
London	16	21	Sh.		25 June 75	30 June 76			T. only		
Lynx	5	444	"		1 July 76	27 July 76					
			Cook 1 Cl		28 July 76						
					13 Jan 77						
London	15	1084			21 Sept 7	12 Oct 77			V. Good		
Flying Fish	17	17			13 Oct 77	19 Oct 77			T. only		
Malabar	16	20	"		20 Oct 77	5 Dec 77			T. only		
D. of Wellington	15ª	33	"		6 Dec 77	7 Jan 78			T. only		
Naval Barracks	15	3655	"		8 Jan 78	14 Jan 78			T. only	Shore	
D. of Wellington	15	3419	"		13 Jan 79	27 Mar 79			Exy		
Impregnable	5	215	"		28 Mch 79	7 Apl 79			Exy		
Lion	5	31	"		8 Apl 79	30 June 81					
Royal Adelaide	16	746	Cook 2Cl		1 July 81				V. Good		
D. of Wellington	15	9476	"		15 Sept 81	22 Sept 81			T. only		
Grappler	5	34	"		23 Sept 81	25 Sept 81			P. only		
Rl. Adelaide	16	963	Cook's Mate		7 Oct 81				Fair		
D. of Wellington	15	9756	"		22 Oct 81	8 Nov 81			T. only		
Eurydice	5	157	"		9 Nov 81	15 Nov 81			V. Good		
	18	61	Cook 1 Cl		16 Nov 81	10 Jan 82			V. Good		
R. Adelaide	16	3239			11 Jan 82						
D. Wellington	15	1713	"		19 May 82	7 Jane 83			V. Good		
Flora A.I	5	43	"		9 April 83	18 May 83			T. only		
D. of Wellington	15	6938	"		19 May 83	10 Sept 83			V. Good		
Penelope	5	840	"		11 Sept 83	26 Oct 83			V.G.	Invalided	Traced P. 2.11.86
					27 Oct 83	31 Jan 84					
					1 Feb 86	8 Oct 86					

Figure 12 Record of Service for Cook 1st Class John Payne (ADM 188/48)

Figure 13   Officers of HMS *Calliope*, 1890 (COPY 1/400)

Figure 14   Training ship and naval cadets at Greenwich, 1891 (COPY 1/400)

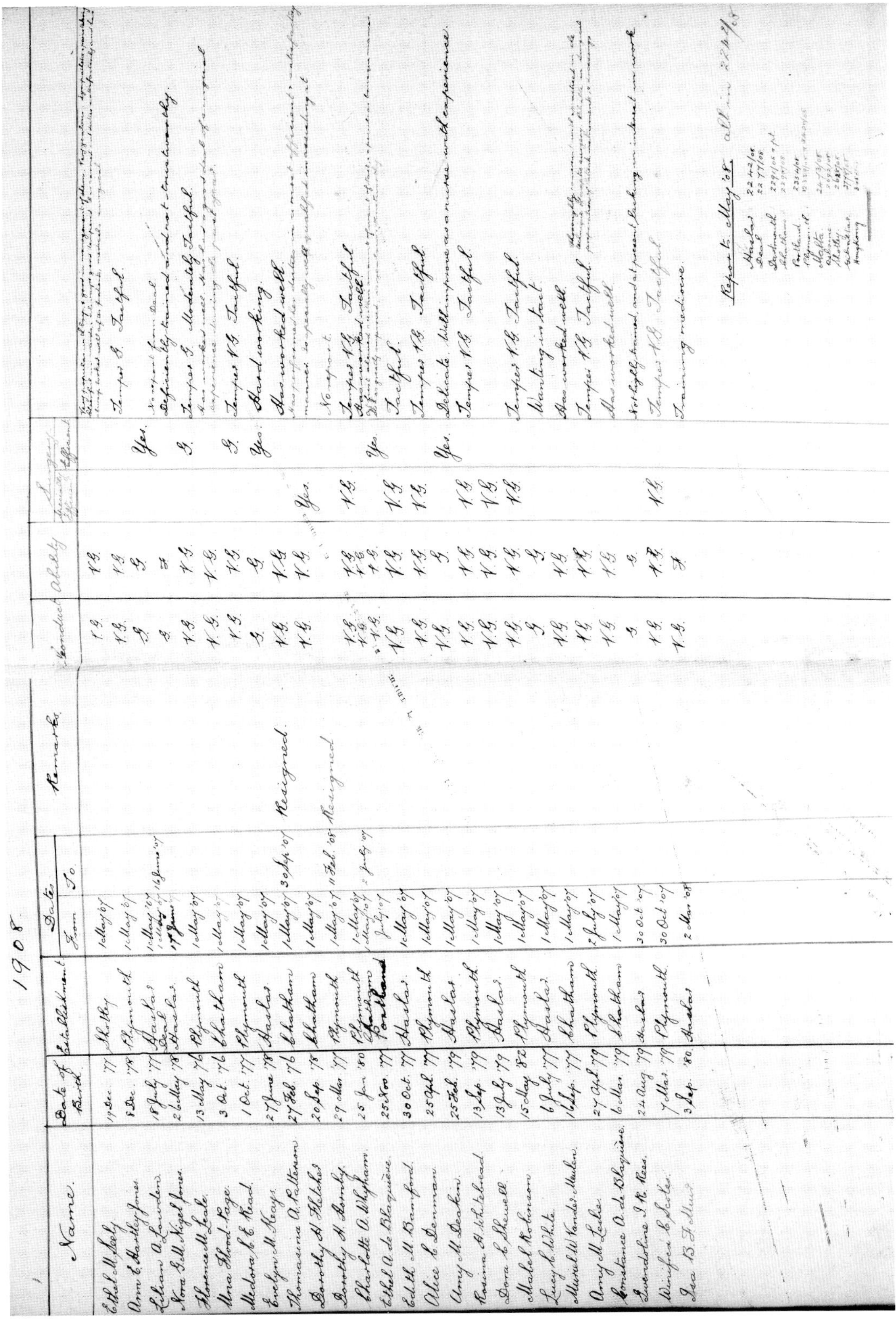

Figure 15   Annual Reports on Nursing Sisters, 1908 (ADM 104/95)

O. No. 7. 7355/7300

192

Sql P.O.7295 Hurt, Bernard Joseph (23) Single   RN 9063.

37 Wood Lane, Shepherd's Bush, London, W.   Motor Driver

20/- Friend, Mrs J. Smith, same address.

N.O.K. Above friend

C.E. Swim. Yeo. E. Grey H. Daw C. Wood.

Measurements. C. 39. W. 34. S. 42 L. 31½ H. 5.9 B. 8. Cp. 7⅞.

One Service joined R.N.A.S. May 1915 - A.M.I. Transferred to Squad 15

Sept 1915 - France and Belgium

1-12-15 Embarked for Russia

Aug.Novr.1916. On detached service in Persia.

Nov.Decr.   On detached service in Dobrudsha.   Hirsova base.
Decr.   On Danube Commission Yacht.s.s.Prince Ferdinand de Roumanie.
Decr.   On detached service in Roumania.   Braila.

            Promoted to Leading Petty Officer. Discipline.
  1917.
25th March. Left Tiraspol Base for detached service on Yacht Prince Ferdinand
19th May.   Transferred to Squadron 2.   de Roumanie.
18th July. Left Tiraspol Base for service in Galicia.   Proskurov.
31st July. Left Proskurov Base for Brovary Base.
17th.Sept. Left Brovary for England on leave.
18/10/17 Arrived in England
22/1/18 Transferred to M.G.C.

Punishments

5-1-1916 "Alexandrovsk" 14 days extra fatigue. reduced to 7 days on account
of good behaviour.

2-2-1916 "Alexandrovsk" sentenced to 14 days cells. to be served on H.M.S.
Albemarle.

Figure 16   Record of Service for Motor Driver Bernard Hurt of the RNAS Russian Armoured
Car Squadron, 1916-1918 (ADM 116/1717)

20 Superannuation & Retirement Pensions contd

Officers	PRO References	Dates	Remarks	Series
Engineers, Boatswains, Gunners, Carpenters, Chaplains	ADM 23/36-41	1871-1881	Engineers & Asst. Engineers only (granted to 1877)	CO
Engineers, Boatswains, Gunners, Carpenters, Coast Guard Wt. Officers	PMG 69	1874-1924	Engineers & Asst. Engineers only (granted to 1877)	CM
Flag Officers, Captains, Commanders, Lieutenants, Sub-Lieutenants, Masters, Surgeons, Pursers, Engineers, Chaplains	PMG 15/79-82	1876-1879		CL
Captains, Commanders, Staff Captains, Staff Commanders	ADM 23/83-88	1878-1899		CQ
Flag Officers, Captains, Commanders, Lieutenants, Sub-Lieutenants, Masters, Surgeons, Pursers, Engineers, Chaplains	PMG 15/88-91	1879-1882		AL
Engineers, Boatswains, Gunners, Carpenters, Coast Guard Wt. Officers, Schoolmasters	ADM 23/101-105	1880-1901	Engineers & Asst. Engineers (granted to 1877)	CO
Flag Officers, Captains, Commanders, Lieutenants, Sub-Lieutenants, Masters, Surgeons, Pursers, Engineers	ADM 22/488-522	1881-1934		CP
Flag Officers, Captains, Commanders, Lieutenants, Sub-Lieutenants, Masters, Surgeons, Pursers, Engineers, Chaplains	PMG 15/97-100	1882-1885		CL

20 Superannuation & Retirement Pensions contd

	PRO References	Dates	Remarks	Series
Pilots	PMG 20/6	1882-1885		AX
Coast Guard	ADM 23/71-75	1884-1902		EP
Yard Officers, Hospital Matrons	ADM 23/78-82	1884-1902		EQ
Nurses	ADM 23/56-70	1884-1902		BO
Flag Officers, Captains, Commanders, Lieutenants, Mates, Sub-Lieutenants, Masters, Surgeons, Pursers, Engineers, Chaplains	PMG 15/106-109	1885-1888		CL
Pilots	PMG 20/8	1885-1888		AX
Flag Officers, Captains, Commanders, Lieutenants, Sub-Lieutenants, Masters, Surgeons, Pursers, Engineers, Chaplains	PMG 15/115-118	1888-1892		CL
Pilots	PMG 20/10	1888-1891		AX
Midshipmen, other Wt. Officers	PMG 69/9-69	1889-1924		CM
Pilots	PMG 20/12	1891-1895		AX
Flag Officers, Captains, Commanders, Lieutenants, Sub-Lieutenants, Masters, Surgeons, Pursers, Engineers, Chaplains	PMG 15/124-127	1892-1896		CL
Pilots	PMG 20/17-20	1895-1911		AX
Flag Officers, Captains, Commanders, Lieutenants, Sub-Lieutenants, Masters, Surgeons, Pursers, Engineers, Chaplains	PMG 15/145-164	1896-1912		CL

20 Superannuation & Retirement Pensions contd

	PRO References	Dates	Remarks	Series
Artificer Engineers	ADM 23/105	1897-1901		CO
Artificer Engineers	PMG 69/13-29	1897-1924		CM
Flag Officers, Captains, Commanders, Naval Ordnance Department	ADM 23/161-167	1899-1927		CQ
Wardmasters	PMG 69/13-29	1900-1924		CM
Wardmasters	ADM 23/105	1900-1901		CO
Engineers, Boatswains, Gunners, Carpenters, Coast Guard Officers, Schoolmasters, Wardmasters, Artificer Engineers	ADM 23/173-179	1901-1931	Engineers & Asst. Engineers only (granted to 1877)	CO
Yard Officers, Hospital Matrons	ADM 23/192-193	1902-1910		EQ
Nursing Sisters	ADM 23/180-191	1902-1926		BO
Coast Guard	ADM 23/194-199	1902-1926		EP
Yard Officers, Hospital Matrons	ADM 23/196-199	1910-1926		EQ
New Wt. ranks	ADM 23/175-179	1910-1931		CO
New Wt. ranks	PMG 69/19-29	1910-1924		CM
QARNNS	ADM 23/164-167	1911-1927		CQ
Flag Officers, Captains, Commanders, Lieutenants, Mates, Sub-Lieutenants, Masters, Surgeons, Pursers, Engineers, Chaplains	PMG 15/170-177	1912-1920		CL
Flag Officers, Captains, Commanders, QARNNS, RFA Masters & Mates, Naval Ordnance Department	ADM 23/172	1927-1932		CQ

21 Service Registers

	PRO References	Dates	Remarks	Series
Flag Officers, Captains, Commanders, Lieutenants	ADM 10/15	1660-1685	(Services)	CR
Flag Officers, Captains, Commanders, Lieutenants	ADM 10/10	1660-1688	(Services)	CR
GH Nurses	ADM 73/83-88	1704-1864		
Surgeons	ADM 104/12-19	1774-1886	(Seniority)	CS
Assistant Surgeons	ADM 104/20-28	1795-1873	(Seniority)	CS
Masters	ADM 6/135-168	c1800-1850	Files	Q
Surgeons	ADM 104/33	1806-1815	(Entries + Services to 1822)	
Surgeons	ADM 11/40	c1808-1813	(Compiled)	
Chaplains	ADM 6/440-441	1812-1880	(Entries)	
Captains, Commanders, Lieutenants	ADM 6/50-52	c1814	(Compiled)	
Engineers	ADM 196/71	1837-1839	(Entries)	CT
Chaplains	ADM 196/68	1837-1860	(Compiled)	
Engineers	ADM 29/105-111	1839-1879	(Entries)	CT
Flag Officers, Captains, Commanders, Lieutenants, Midshipmen, Masters	ADM 11/1	c1840	(Compiled)	
Surgeons	ADM 196/8	c1840-1850	(Compiled + Entries)	CU
Surgeons	ADM 196/9-10	1841-1895	(Entries)	CU
Flag Officers	ADM 11/12	1843	(Compiled)	
Captains	ADM 11/12-13	1843-1844	(Compiled)	
Commanders	ADM 11/11-12	1843-1846	(Compiled)	
Flag Officers, Captains, Commanders, Lieutenants, Mates, Sub-Lieutenants	ADM 196/1-7	c1843-1875	(Compiled)	CV

21 Service Registers contd

	PRO References	Dates	Remarks	Series
Masters, Surgeons, Pursers	ADM 196/1	c1843-1875	(Compiled + Entries)	CV
Pharmacists	ADM 104/159-160	1845-1957	(Entries + Services)	
Flag Officers, Captains, Commanders, Lieutenants, Mates, Sub-Lieutenants, Midshipmen, Cadets	ADM 196/36-37	1846-1867	(Compiled + Entries)	CW
Lieutenants	ADM 11/11	1846	(Compiled)	
Masters, Surgeons, Pursers	ADM 196/74-79	1848-1873	(Services)	CX
Boatswains, Gunners, Carpenters, Chaplains	ADM 196/74-76	1848-1855	(Services)	CX
Carpenters	ADM 29/114-115	1848-1912	(Entries + Services)	
Surgeons	ADM 105/75-76	1848-1855	(Compiled + Services)	CY
Surgeons	ADM 104/31-42	1850-1894	(Compiled + Services)	CY
Pursers	ADM 196/11-12	1852-1884	(Compiled + Services)	CZ
Foreign Officers	ADM 7/912	1852-1898	(Entries)	
Masters	ADM 196/22	1853-1872	(Entries)	
Boatswains, Gunners, Carpenters	ADM 196/29-32	1855-1890	(Entries)	DA
Masters	ADM 196/77-81	1856-1882	(Compiled + Entries)	CX
Engineers	ADM 196/23	1856-1882	(Compiled + Entries)	DB
Engineers	ADM 196/24-25	1858-1886	(Entries)	DB
Masters	ADM 196/21	1859	(Compiled)	
Staff/Fleet Surgeons	ADM 104/29	1859-1886	(Seniority)	CS
Flag Officers, Captains, Commanders, Lieutenants, Mates, Sub-Lieutenants, Midshipmen, Cadets	ADM 196/17-20	1860-1878	(Entries)	DC
Boatswains	ADM 29/116-119	1860-1912 1912 only)	(Entries + Services to	EO

21 Service Registers contd

	PRO References	Dates	Remarks	Series
Ratings RNR	BT 164	1860-1908	(Entries)	DD
Flag Officers, Captains, Commanders, Lieutenants	ADM 196/13-16	1861	(Compiled)	DC
Lieutenants RNR	ADM 240/3-6	1862-1901	(Seniority)	DE
Sub-Lieutenants RNR	ADM 240/8-12	1862-1897	(Seniority)	DE
Masters	ADM 196/73	1864-1874	(Compiled + Entries)	
Engineers RNR	ADM 240/29-31	1865-1907	(Seniority)	DE
Flag Officers, Captains, Commanders, Lieutenants, Sub-Lieutenants, Midshipmen, Cadets	ADM 196/38-56	1867-1907	(Entries)	CW
Engine Room Artificers	ADM 29/123	1868-1871		
Medical Officers, Nurses & employees	ADM 305/80	1870-1890	RNH Haslar	
Midshipmen RNR	ADM 240/19-24	1873-1898	(Seniority)	DE
Surgeons	ADM 196/80-81	1873-1882	(Compiled + Entries)	CX
Pursers	ADM 196/80-81	1873-1882	(Services)	CX
Ratings	ADM 188/5-244	1873-1891	(Entries)	DF
Chief Engine Room Artificers	ADM 29/124	1877-1888		
Medical Officers, Nurses & employees	ADM 305/81	1877-1917	RNH Hong Kong	
Masters, Pursers	ADM 196/82	1881-1891	(Entries)	CZ
Schoolmasters	ADM 196/32	1882-1890	(Seniority)	
Nursing Sisters	ADM 104/43	1884-1909	(Entries + Services)	
Coast Guard Officers	ADM 175/103-107	1886-1919	(Seniority)	DG
Signal Boatswains	ADM 29/120	1890-1912 (1912 only)	(Entries + Services to	
Pursers, Chaplains	ADM 6/442-444	1891-1916	(Entries)	CZ

21 Service Registers contd

	PRO References	Dates	Remarks	Series
Flag Officers, Captains	ADM 196/86-94	1893-1944	(Seniority)	EU
Coast Guard Ratings	ADM 175/82-90	1900-1923		DH
Lieutenants	ADM 196/84	1903-1912	(Promotions) Cd. Gunners	
Boatswains, Gunners, Carpenters	ADM 196/34-35	1903ff	(Services)	
Flag Officers, Captains, Commanders, Lieutenants, Sub-Lieutenants, Midshipmen, Naval Cadets	ADM 196/96	1906-1916	(Entries + special promotions and transfers from RNR)	CW
RNAS Officers	ADM 273	1914-1918	(Services)	ET
Ratings	ADM 116/1717	1915-1918	RNAS Russian Armoured Cars	
Pursers, Chaplains	ADM 196/85	1916-1922	(Entries)	CZ
WRNS Officers	ADM 318	1917-1919	(Entries + Services)	FC
Coast Guard Officers	ADM 175/109-110	1919-1947	(Seniority)	DG
Coast Guard/Shore Signal Service Ratings	ADM 175/111	1921-1929		

22 Succession Books

	PRO References	Dates	Remarks	Series
Captains, Commanders, Lieutenants, Pursers, Boatswains, Gunners, Carpenters, Cooks	ADM 6/425-426	1673-1688		
Captains, Commanders	ADM 7/655	1688-1725		CR
Midshipmen Ordinary, Volunteers per Order, Chaplains, Masters at Arms, Schoolmasters	ADM 6/427	1699-1756		DI

22 Succession Books contd

	PRO References	Dates	Remarks	Series
Masters, Surgeons, Sailmakers	ADM 106/2896-2897	1733-1755		DJ
Flag Officers	ADM 12/15	1742-1808	C-in-C	
Flag Officers	ADM 10/9	1755-1848	C-in-C	
Midshipmen Ordinary, Chaplains, Masters at Arms, Schoolmasters	ADM 6/185	1757-1824		DI
Pursers, Boatswains, Gunners, Carpenters	ADM 106/2898	1764-1784		DK
Masters, Sailmakers	ADM 106/2899-2901	1770-1807		DJ
Surgeons	ADM 106/2899-2900	1770-1798		DJ
Captains, Commanders, Lieutenants	ADM 11/65-72	1780-1847		DL
Pursers, Boatswains, Gunners, Carpenters	ADM 11/65-71	1780-1848		DL
Captains, Commanders, Lieutenants, Masters, Surgeons, Pursers, Boatswains, Gunners, Carpenters, Chaplains	ADM 7/762	1782-1783	East Indies	
Pursers, Boatswains, Gunners, Carpenters	ADM 106/2902-2906	1785-1831		DK
Yard Officers	ADM 106/2902	1785-1799		DK
Surgeons	ADM 102/851-852	1789-1807		
Caulkers	ADM 106/2900	1790-1798		
Surgeons & Surgeon's Mates	ADM 104/6-7	1790-1822		DJ
Captains, Commanders, Lieutenants	ADM 6/58	1795-1796		DJ
Captains, Commanders, Lieutenants	ADM 11/56-57	1797-1801		
Captains, Commanders, Lieutenants	ADM 6/57	1798-1799		DM

22 Succession Books contd

	PRO References	Dates	Remarks	Series
Ropemakers	ADM 106/2901	1799–1807		DJ
Pursers, Boatswains, Gunners, Carpenters	ADM 6/192	1800–1812		DN
Mates, Midshipmen	ADM 6/175	1802–1803	Admiralty Orders	
Captains, Commanders, Lieutenants Sub-Lieutenants	ADM 6/59	1803–1804		
	ADM 11/19	1805–1810		
Captains, Commanders, Lieutenants	ADM 11/58–63	1806–1848		DM
Surgeons	ADM 104/1–2	1809–1817	Hospital Staff	
Pursers, Boatswains, Gunners, Carpenters	ADM 11/31–33	1812–1839		DN
Mates, Midshipmen, Cadets	ADM 11/23–30	1815–1853		DO
Yard Officers	ADM 106/2905–2906	1815–1831		DK
Coast Guard Officers & Ratings	ADM 175/1–73	1816–1918		DP
Supernumerary Clerks	ADM 11/25–29	1821–1848		DO
Master's Assistants & 2nd Class Volunteers	ADM 6/169	1824–1829		DQ
Master's Assistants & 2nd Class Volunteers	ADM 11/20	1829–1839		DQ
Masters, Surgeons, Chaplains, Cooks	ADM 11/71	1832–1848		DL
Engineers	ADM 11/49	1835–1844		
Clerks	ADM 11/47	1838–1849		
Master's Assistants	ADM 11/21	1839–1849		DQ
Engineers	ADM 11/48	1841–1849		
Flag Officers, Captains, Commanders, Lieutenants	ADM 11/73–79	1846–1903		DM

22 Succession Books contd

	PRO References	Dates	Remarks	Series
Mates, Sub-Lieutenants, Midshipmen, Cadets	ADM 11/81-87	1853-1888		DO
Engineers, Boatswains, Gunners, Carpenters	ADM 29/122	1854-1861		
Surgeons	ADM 104/88-94	1870-1924	Inc. hospitals	DR
Masters, Surgeons, Pursers, Chaplains, Coast Guard Chief Officers & Mates	ADM 7/925-927	1870-1884		
Boatswains, Gunners, Carpenters	ADM 29/125-130	1872-1896		DS
Engineers	ADM 29/126-130	1882-1896		DS
Captains, Commanders, Lieutenants, Sub-Lieutenants, Surgeons, Pursers, Engineers, Boatswains, Gunners, Carpenters, Chaplains	ADM 8/173-174	1903-1909		
Flag Officers	ADM 6/461	1913-1919	Inc. staffs	
QARNNS, Wardmasters	ADM 104/96	1921-1939	In hospitals	

23 Surveys

	PRO References	Dates	Remarks	Series
Boatswains, Gunners, Carpenters	ADM 11/35-37	1816-1818		DT
Captains, Commanders, Lieutenants	ADM 6/66	1817	Strays	DU
Captains, Commanders, Lieutenants	ADM 10/2-5	1817	Indexes	DU
Captains, Commanders, Lieutenants	ADM 9/2-17	1817		DU
Flag Officers, Captains, Commanders, Lieutenants	ADM 6/73-83	1822	Age	DV
Masters	ADM 106/3517	1822	Age	DV
Flag Officers	ADM 10/1	1828	Index	

23 Surveys contd

	PRO References	Dates	Remarks	Series
Flag Officers	ADM 6/66	1828	Strays	
Flag Officers	ADM 9/1	1828		
Commanders, Lieutenants	ADM 6/83-85	1831	Age	DV
Masters	ADM 11/2-3	1833-1835		
Pursers	ADM 6/193-196	1834		
Flag Officers, Captains, Commanders, Lieutenants, Mates	ADM 9/18-61	1846		EN
Flag Officers, Captains, Commanders, Lieutenants, Mates	ADM 10/6-7	1846	Index	EN
Mates, Masters	ADM 11/10	1847	Age	
Masters	ADM 11/7-8	1851		EN
Masters	ADM 10/6-7	1851	Indexes	EN
Pursers	ADM 11/42-43	1852		
Masters	ADM 11/9	1855 & 1861		
Pursers	ADM 11/44	1859		

24 Seniority Lists

	PRO References	Dates	Remarks	Series
Captains, Commanders	ADM 7/549	1652-1737	Annotated	CR
Captains	ADM 6/424	1673-1754	Annotated	CR
Captains, Commanders	ADM 10/10	1688-1746	Annotated	CR
Captains, Commanders, Lieutenants	ADM 118/1-185	1717-1846		DW
RNA Scholars	ADM 6/427	1733-1756		DI
Flag Officers	ADM 118/2-185	1743-1846		DW
RNA Scholars	ADM 6/185	1757-1824		DI

24 *Seniority Lists contd*

	PRO References	Dates	Remarks	Series
Masters	ADM 118/186-189	1780-1784		DX
Surgeons	ADM 104/51-55	1780-1784		DY
Surgeons	ADM 104/56	1787		DY
Masters	ADM 118/190	1791		DX
Surgeons	ADM 118/191	1791		DY
Surgeons	ADM 104/57-79	1796-1817		DY
Flag Officers, Captains, Commanders, Lieutenants	ADM 118/337-352	1800-1824	(Not continuous)	DW
RNC Scholars	ADM 1/3506-3521	1809-1839	Index in Research Enquiries Room	
Masters	ADM 6/132	1809	(Compiled) Annotated	DZ
Pursers	ADM 118/192-207	1810-1822		DZ
Boatswains, Gunners, Carpenters	ADM 118/192-201	1810-1817		EA
Surgeons	ADM 118/353	1813		DY
RNC Scholars	ADM 30/21	1817-1832		
Pursers	ADM 118/354-355	1817 & 1820		DZ
Boatswains, Gunners, Carpenters	ADM 118/354	1817		EA
Surgeons	ADM 104/80	1820-1823		DY
Boatswains, Gunners, Carpenters	ADM 118/205	1820		EA
Boatswains, Gunners, Carpenters	ADM 118/355	1820		EA
Boatswains, Gunners, Carpenters	ADM 118/208	1827		EA
Masters, Surgeons, Pursers	ADM 118/209	1829		DX-DZ
Masters	ADM 118/210-212	1832		DX

24 Seniority Lists contd

	PRO References	Dates	Remarks	Series
Surgeons	ADM 118/210-211	1832		DY
Pursers	ADM 118/213-215	1832		DZ
Pursers	ADM 118/210-211	1832		DZ
Pursers	ADM 118/218-220	1833-1834		DZ
Boatswains, Gunners, Carpenters	ADM 118/356	1833		EA
Boatswains, Gunners, Carpenters	ADM 118/216-217	1833		EA
Surgeons	ADM 118/219-220	1834		DY
Masters	ADM 118/219-221	1834-1836		DX
Surgeons, Pursers	ADM 118/221	1836		DY, DZ
Boatswains, Gunners, Carpenters	ADM 118/222	1836		EA
Masters, Surgeons, Pursers	ADM 118/223-225	1839		DX-DZ
Boatswains, Gunners, Carpenters	ADM 118/226	1839		EA
Masters	ADM 118/227-228	1841		DX
Surgeons	ADM 118/357-358	1841-1842		DY
Pursers	ADM 118/227-228	1841		DZ
Mates, Masters, Surgeons, Pursers	ADM 118/183-185	1844-1846		DW-DZ
Boatswains, Gunners, Carpenters	ADM 118/229	1844		EA
Chaplains	ADM 118/183-185	1844-1846	(Seniority)	DW
Sub-Lieutenants RNR	ADM 240/13-17	1862-1906		
Surgeons	ADM 104/81-84	1868		DY
Surgeons	ADM 104/85	1878		DY
Surgeons	ADM 104/86-87	1886		DY

	PRO References	Dates	Remarks	Series
24 Seniority Lists contd				
Lieutenants RNR	ADM 240/7	1902-1907	(Seniority)	
Commanders RNR	ADM 240/1	1904-1907	(Seniority)	
Flag Officers, Captains, Commanders, Lieutenants, Mates, Sub-Lieutenants, Surgeons, Pursers, Engineers, Boatswains, Gunners, Carpenters, Chaplains, Other Wt. & Cd. Wt. Officers	ADM 177/1-18	1914-1919	+ Other Navy Lists	X
Cadets	ADM 203/104-198	1931-1968	RNC Dartmouth	FD
Flag Officers, Captains, Commanders, Lieutenants, Sub-Lieutenants, Surgeons, Pursers, Engineers, Boatswains, Gunners, Carpenters, Chaplains, Other Wt. & Cd. Wt. Officers	ADM 177/19-61	1939-1945	+ Other Navy Lists	X
25 Unfit for Service				
Lieutenants	ADM 6/173	1804-1811		
26 Warrants				
Masters, Surgeons, Pursers, Boatswains, Gunners, Carpenters, Chaplains, Masters at Arms, Yard Officers	ADM 6/3-32	1695-1815		G
Cooks	ADM 6/3-8	1695-1704		G

26 Warrants contd

	PRO References	Dates	Remarks	Series
Chaplains, Masters at Arms	ADM 6/427	1699-1756		DI
Masters, Surgeons, Pursers, Boatswains, Gunners, Carpenters, Chaplains, Cooks, Masters at Arms	ADM 1/5115/10	1742	Mediterranean	
Pursers, Boatswains, Carpenters	ADM 6/63	1742-1768	Abroad	
Chaplains, Masters at Arms	ADM 6/61	1742-1768	Abroad	
Masters, Surgeons, Pursers, Boatswains, Gunners, Carpenters	ADM 6/33-38	1744-1798	Admiralty outport fee books	H
Armourers	WO 54/685	1755-1762		
Chaplains, Masters at Arms	ADM 6/185	1757-1824		DI
Masters, Surgeons, Pursers, Boatswains, Gunners, Carpenters, Chaplains, Cooks, Masters at Arms	ADM 1/5116/12	1757-1770	North America & West Indies	
Masters, Surgeons, Pursers, Boatswains, Gunners, Carpenters, Chaplains, Cooks, Masters at Arms	ADM 1/5117/1	1769-1773	West Indies	
Masters, Surgeons, Pursers, Boatswains, Gunners, Carpenters, Chaplains, Cooks, Masters at Arms	ADM 6/64-65	1787-1805	Abroad	
Sailmakers, Caulkers, Coopers, Ropemakers	ADM 6/197	1798-1831		
Surgeons, Pursers, Boatswains, Gunners, Carpenters	ADM 6/191	1800-1815		
Yard Officers	ADM 11/18	1803-1815		
Pursers, Boatswains, Gunners, Chaplains, Masters at Arms	ADM 6/53	1804-1806		

26 Warrants contd

	PRO References	Dates	Remarks	Series
Yard Officers	ADM 11/14-17	1804-1817		
Pursers	ADM 11/50	1810-1814		
2nd Masters	ADM 6/133	1816-1833		
Masters, Surgeons, Pursers, Boatswains, Gunners, Carpenters, Chaplains, Cooks, Masters at Arms	ADM 6/68-72	1824-1846	Abroad	
Mates	ADM 11/22	1829-1860		I
Masters, Surgeons, Pursers Boatswains, Gunners, Carpenters	ADM 6/48-49	1832-1849	Admiralty outport fee books	H
Mates	ADM 6/184	1840-1845		
Gunners	ADM 6/61	1842-1868	Abroad	

27 Wills

	PRO References	Dates	Remarks	Series
Ratings	ADM 48	1786-1882		EB
Ratings	ADM 44	1800-1860		EC
Ratings	HCA 30/455-458	1805-1807	Certificates of intestacy	
Flag Officers, Captains, Commanders, Lieutenants, Mates, Masters, Surgeons, Pursers, Engineers, Boatswains, Gunners, Carpenters, Chaplains, Cooks	ADM 45	1830-1860		ED
All Officers & Widows	PMG 50/1-9	1836-1914	Probate & administration	FE

	PRO References	Dates	Remarks	Series
28 Addresses				
Flag Officers, Captains, Commanders, Lieutenants, Mates, Masters, Surgeons, Pursers, Chaplains	PMG 73/2	1837		
29 Schools Papers				
Captains, Commanders, Lieutenants, Mates, Sub-Lieutenants, Midshipmen, Masters, Surgeons, Pursers, Boatswains, Gunners, Carpenters, Chaplains, Cooks, Masters at Arms, Ratings	ADM 73/154-389	1728-1861		EE
Captains, Commanders, Lieutenants, Mates, Sub-Lieutenants, Midshipmen, Masters, Surgeons, Pursers, Boatswains, Gunners, Carpenters, Chaplains, Cooks, Masters at Arms, Ratings	ADM 73/404-406	1728-1828		EF
Captains, Commanders, Lieutenants, Mates, Sub-Lieutenants, Midshipmen, Masters, Surgeons, Pursers, Boatswains, Gunners, Carpenters, Chaplains, Cooks, Masters at Arms, Ratings	ADM 73/416-417	1728-1821		EF

29 *Schools Papers contd*

PRO References	Dates	Remarks	Series
ADM 73/391-397	1803-1861	Lower School	EK
ADM 73/410-411	1805-1861	Lower School	
ADM 73/442-443	1805-1840	Lower School, Girls	
ADM 73/412-414	1815-1861	Upper School	EF
ADM 73/440-441	1826-1841	Lower School, Girls	EJ
ADM 73/425	1828-1861	Upper School	

Captains, Commanders, Lieutenants, Mates, Midshipmen, Masters, Surgeons, Pursers, Boatswains, Gunners, Carpenters, Chaplains, Cooks, Masters at Arms, Ratings

Captains, Commanders, Lieutenants, Mates, Midshipmen, Masters, Surgeons, Pursers, Boatswains, Gunners, Carpenters, Chaplains, Cooks, Masters at Arms, Ratings

Captains, Commanders, Lieutenants, Mates, Midshipmen, Masters, Surgeons, Pursers, Boatswains, Gunners, Carpenters, Chaplains, Cooks, Masters at Arms, Ratings

Captains, Commanders, Lieutenants, Mates, Midshipmen, Masters, Surgeons, Pursers, Boatswains, Gunners, Carpenters, Chaplains, Cooks, Masters at Arms, Ratings

Captains, Commanders, Lieutenants, Mates, Midshipmen, Masters, Surgeons, Pursers, Boatswains, Gunners, Carpenters, Chaplains, Cooks, Ratings

Captains, Commanders, Lieutenants, Mates, Masters, Surgeons, Pursers, Chaplains

29 Schools Papers contd

	PRO References	Dates	Remarks	Series
Captains, Commanders, Lieutenants, Mates, Masters, Surgeons, Pursers, Chaplains	ADM 73/399	1828-1837	Lower School	
Captains, Commanders, Lieutenants, Mates, Midshipmen, Masters, Surgeons, Pursers, Boatswains, Gunners, Carpenters, Chaplains, Cooks, Ratings	ADM 73/415	1832-1844	Upper School	EG
Engineers	ADM 73/411	1837-1865	Lower School	
Engineers	ADM 73/413-414	1837-1861	Upper School	EF
Engineers	ADM 73/443	1837-1840	Lower School, Girls	
Engineers	ADM 73/395-397	1837-1861	Lower School	EK
Engineers	ADM 73/415	1837-1844	Upper School	EG
Engineers	ADM 73/154-389	1837-1861		EE
Engineers	ADM 73/441	1837-1841	Lower Schools, Girls	EJ
Captains, Commanders, Lieutenants, Mates, Sub-Lieutenants, Midshipmen, Masters, Surgeons, Pursers, Engineers, Boatswains, Gunners, Carpenters, Chaplains, Cooks, Ratings	ADM 73/398	1844-1861	Upper School	EG
Ratings, Nurses	ADM 73/90	1844-1868	Infants' School, In-Pensioners & Staff	
Captains, Commanders, Lieutenants, Mates, Masters, Surgeons, Pursers, Engineers, Chaplains	ADM 73/400	1846-1860	Upper School	
Engineers	ADM 73/425	1847-1861	Upper School	

29 Schools Papers contd

	PRO References	Dates	Remarks	Series
Boatswains, Gunners, Carpenters, Cooks	ADM 73/400	1850-1860	Upper School	
Boatswains, Gunners, Carpenters, Cooks	ADM 73/425	1850-1861	Upper School	
Boatswains, Gunners, Carpenters, Cooks, Ratings	ADM 161/1	1865-1870	Lower School	EK
Boatswains, Gunners, Carpenters, Cooks, Ratings	ADM 161/2	1867-1881	Upper School	EG
Boatswains, Gunners, Carpenters, Ratings	ADM 161/3-19	1870-1930	Lower School	EK
Other Wt. Officers	ADM 161/4-19	1881-1930	Lower School	EK

30 Entries

	PRO References	Dates	Remarks	Series
Ratings	ADM 30/63/1	1744-1745	From Leghorn	
Ratings	ADM 30/63/4	1781	From St. Lucia	
Ratings	ADM 30/63/5	1790	From Greenock	
Ratings	ADM 30/63/11	c1792-1800	From Falmouth	
Ratings	ADM 30/63/7	1794-1795	From Waterford	
Ratings	ADM 30/63/8	1795	From Isle of Wight	
Ratings	ADM 7/361	1795	From London	
Ratings	ADM 30/63/9	1796-1799	From Edinburgh	
Ratings	ADM 7/362	1797	From Essex	
Ratings	ADM 30/63/10	1803	From Londonderry	
GH Nurses	ADM 6/239	1817-1831		

30 Entries contd

	PRO References	Dates	Remarks	Series
Ratings	ADM 1/5123/25	1824	Impressed smugglers	
Stokers	ADM 29/107	1834-1846		
Engineer's Boys	ADM 29/106	1839-1853		
Ratings	ADM 188/1-4	1853-1855	For Continuous Service	
Ratings	ADM 139	1853-1872	For Continuous Service	EL

31 Discharges

	PRO References	Dates	Remarks	Series
Ratings	ADM 1/5118/5	1781-1783	Unfit for Service	
Ratings	ADM 1/5120/19	1792	Unfit for Service from Haslar Hospital	
Ratings	ADM 6/67	1812-1815	Plymouth, by Habeas Corpus	
Coast Guard Ratings	ADM 175/102	1858-1868		
Coast Guard Chief Officers and Ratings	ADM 175/91-96	1919		

32 Musters

	PRO References	Dates	Remarks	Series
Ratings	ADM 30/45	1779-1782	Small vessels in America	
Ratings	ADM 30/63/3	1780	Prison ships at New York	
Ratings	ADM 30/63/6	1793-1798	Maltese	

	PRO References	Dates	Remarks	Series
32 Musters contd				
Sea Fencibles	ADM 28/1-144	1798-1810		
French Pilots	ADM 1/5121/10	1802		
Ratings	ADM 30/46	1813-1814	Canadian Lakes Squadron	
Ratings	ADM 30/47	1808-1815	Heligoland Harbour-master's boat's crew	
Ratings	ADM 30/26	1819-1820	Kroomen	
33 Miscellaneous				
Medical Officers' children	ADM 305/86	1829-1862	RNH Haslar, Baptismal Register	
Pursers	SP 18/119, 151, 177, 198, 218, 225	1655-1660	Bonds	

APPENDIX II

Service Records in Series

Series A

A series of registers of Pursers, Boatswains, Gunners and Carpenters applying for employment and promotion, or applied for by senior officers, with notes of the results, and of the applicants' last ships. They are in chronological order without indexes. From 1793 Chaplains are included.

Dates	PRO References
1770-1783	ADM 6/187
1793-1790	ADM 6/188
1790-1795	ADM 6/189

Series B

A series of rough registers of Lieutenants applying for employment, or applied for by Admirals and patrons, with the results for their applications. There are notes of the officers' previous ships, and of their addresses. The volumes overlap slightly in date. There are internal indexes.

Dates	Remarks	PRO References
1799-1805		ADM 6/170
1804-1813		ADM 6/171
1812-1818	Arranged by port	ADM 6/172

Series C

A series of registers of nominations for appointments of officers and ratings to the Coast Guard.

Nos	Dates	Remarks	PRO References	Indexes
1-1126	1819-1821	England		
	1822-1824	Scotland	ADM 175/74	
1-291, 1-45	1820-1824	Ireland		
1127-1523	1821-1822	England	ADM 175/75	
1-823	1823-1826	England	ADM 175/76	ADM 175/97

(continued)

(continued)

Nos	Dates	Remarks	PRO References	Indexes
824-3970	1827-1832	England	ADM 175/77	ADM 175/97
3973-7698	1833-1841	England	ADM 175/78	ADM 175/97
1-4629	1842-1856	England }	ADM 175/79 ADM 175/80	ADM 175/98
4630-9733	1857-1866	England		ADM 175/98
100-1799	1858-1862	Officers		
1-1024	1822-1829	Ireland	ADM 175/81	

Series D

These are entry books in chronological order of Admiralty Orders to officers to act as commanding officers of ships and appointing Lieutenants to the Sea Fencibles, Cutters, tenders, signal stations, dockyards and the Impress Service. The volumes are indexed internally.

Dates	PRO References
1804-1805	ADM 11/14
1805-1808	ADM 11/15
1809-1813	ADM 11/16
1814-1815	ADM 11/17

Series E

A small number of junior officers of foreign navies were attached to the Royal Navy for training, and lists of them were included in these volumes.

Dates	PRO References
1830-1853	ADM 11/27-30
1853-1858	ADM 11/81

Series F

These volumes were known collectively as the Black Book, in which were entered the names of all sea and naval officers noted as not to be employed again on account of misconduct. The books are arranged by the rank of the offender, and for each rank in chronological order. ADM 12/27E is a normal index to the whole.

Vols	Dates	PRO References
1	1741-1793	ADM 12/27B
2	1794-1807	ADM 12/27C
3	1807-1815	ADM 12/27D

Series G

This is the principle series of records kept by the Admiralty of all Commissions, Warrants and Orders issued by both the Admiralty and other Boards. The recipients include yard officers. Commissions and Warrants issued by commanders-in-chief abroad are not included, but Admiralty confirmations of them are. The volumes are in strict chronological order and unindexed, but there is a typescript in the PRO Research Enquiries Room to ADM 6/3-15, and a card index to ADM 6/15-16 and 22-23

Dates	PRO References
1695-1742	ADM 6/3-15
1742-1745	ADM 6/16
1745-1779	ADM 6/17-21
1779-1789	ADM 6/22-23
1789-1815	ADM 6/24-32

Series H

These are registers, in tabular form, of Commissions and Warrants sent out from the Admiralty to officers at outports or overseas, on which the customary fees had not yet been paid. The registers are in chronological order of dispatch of the Commissions or Warrants (not of the dates of the documents themselves) and are unindexed. From 1744 to 1798 each volume also includes copies of Admiralty out-letters relating to the issue of Commissions and Warrants.

Dates	Remarks	PRO References
1744-1798	plus out-letters	ADM 6/33-38
(1799-1810)	*wanting*	
1802-1827	Commissions only	ADM 6/46-47
(1828-1831)	*wanting*	
1832-1849		ADM 6/48-49

Series I

Two registers of young officers who had passed their qualifying examinations to become Lieutenants, with the dates of their actual promotion added. Until 1860 the officers are neatly all Mates, thereafter Sub-Lieutenants. The registers give some ages and dates of births, and details of marks obtained in the examinations. There are internal indexes.

Dates of Passing	PRO References
1829-1865	ADM 11/22
1865-1881	ADM 11/89

Series J

This series consist of reports by captains on Midshipmen, Mates and other candidates for Lieutenants' commissions, assessing their characters and abilities, giving their ages and previous services, and noting when, or if, they received commissions. ADM 6/180 continues the series, but is based on personal memorials from those not then at sea. It also includes some Lieutenants and Masters. There are no indexes.

Dates	PRO References
1814-1816	ADM 6/176-179
1814-1816	ADM 6/180

Series K

These are original reports form the Victualling Board (at that time responsible for the navel medical service), to the Admiralty on questions referred to them concerning the pay, half pay or promotion of Surgeons. There are internal indexes to each piece.

Date	PRO References
1817-1832	ADM 105/1-9

Series L

Theses are drafts and notes kept by the Medical Director-General of the Navy of submissions made by him to the Second Naval Lord of the names of Surgeons for promotion or particular appointments. They include details of the previous services, character and professional abilities of the candidates. All except the first piece have internal indexes.

Dates	PRO References
1845-1866	ADM 104/45
1867-1873	ADM 104/46
1874-1878	ADM 104/47
1878-1888	ADM 104/48
1888-1912	ADM 104/49
1912-1926	ADM 104/50

Series M

A series of registers kept in N Branch, the Second Naval Lord's department, of candidates for Service Nominations as Naval Cadet, 2nd Lieutenant RMLI or Assistant Clerk. These nominations were reserved for the sons of officers who had long service in the rank of Commander or above, or had died in service. The registers give the address, income and services of the candidates' fathers. They are indexed internally.

Dates	Remarks	PRO References
1882-1892		ADM 6/448
1890-1905	Assistant Clerk only	ADM 6/449
1891-1902	Naval Cadets & Lieuts. RMLI only	ADM 6/450
1901-1905	Naval Cadets only	ADM 6/451

Series N

A series of registers kept in the First Lord's Private Office of applicants for nominations to naval cadetships. The first relates the 'Old Scheme' in which candidates entered at the age of fifteen, the remainder to the 'Selborne Scheme' in which they entered at thirteen. The registers give the names, ages and schools of the candidates, and the professions of their fathers. There are internal indexes.

Dates	Remarks	PRO References
1898-1905	Old Scheme	ADM 6/464
1903-1907	Selborne Scheme	ADM 6/465
1908-1913	Selborne Scheme	ADM 6/466
1913-1917	Selborne Scheme	ADM 6/467

Series O

These are the original certificates issued to young gentlemen passing for Lieutenant. They give the fact and date of passing, with a stereotyped list of qualifications, and a summary of each examinee's service to date. They usually state the applicants' ages and sometimes include supporting documents such as baptismal certificates. From 1744 to 1780 they include officers passing overseas. The certificates are bound roughly in alphabetical order within each year, but the volumes overlap.

Dates	Remarks	PRO References
1744-1747		ADM 6/86
(1748-1752)	*wanting*	
1753-1778		ADM 6/87
(1779)	*wanting*	
1780		ADM 6/88
1781-1819		ADM 6/89-116
1788-1818	overseas only	ADM 6/117-118

Series P

These are papers assembled by Greenwich Hospital concerning applications by former ratings and Marines for admission into the Hospital as In-Pensioners. They consist largely of Certificates of Service issued by the Navy Pay Office and are arranged in alphabetical order. Though the certificates were issued from 1790, the services described go back at least forty years earlier.

Letters	Dates	PRO References
A-Z	1790-1865	ADM 73/1-35

Series Q

These are examples of an unusual method of keeping service records in individual files or dossiers. They appear to have been compiled in the 1830s and 1840s, and contain Passing Certificates, Certificates of Service both before and after being warranted, and a variety of correspondence and certificates, all relating to Masters. The series covers approximately the period 1800-1850, and is arranged in alphabetical order.

Letters	*PRO References*
A-Z	ADM 6/135-268

Series R

These entry books were kept in the Navy Pay Office to record details of Certificates of Service issued in respect of young gentlemen wishing to qualify as Lieutenants. There are also a few certificates entered of officers already commissioned. The books are indexed internally.

Dates	*PRO References*
1802-1848	ADM 107/71-75

Series S

These are entry books kept by the Navy Pay Office of Certificates of Service of Boatswains issued to support claims for pension. They give a summary statement of services to the date of issue. There are internal indexes, and an index to the series, ADM 29/97-104.

Vols	*Dates*	*PRO References*
4	1817-1839	ADM 29/4
23	1840-1870	ADM 29/23
121	1870-1873	ADM 29/121

Series T

These are entry books kept by the Navy Pay Office of Certificates of Service of Gunners issued to support claims for pension. They give a summary statement of services to the date of issue. There are internal indexes, and an index to the series, ADM 29/97-104.

Vols	*Dates*	*PRO References*
3	1817-1839	ADM 29/3
24	1840-1871	ADM 29/24
121	1870-1873	ADM 29/121

Series U

These are entry books kept by the Navy Pay Office of Certificates of Service of Carpenters issued to support claims for pension. They give a summary statement of services to the date of issue. There are internal indexes, and an index to the series, ADM 29/97-104.

Vols	Dates	Remarks	PRO References
5	1817-1833		ADM 29/5
6	1834-1853		ADM 29/6
	(1854-1869)	wanting	
121	1870-1873		ADM 29/121

Series V

These are entry books kept by the Navy Pay Office of Certificates of Service issued to support ratings' claims for pensions, gratuities, or medals. They give a summary statement of services, except for those men, entering the Navy from 1853, who served only on Continuous Service. In these cases the books give only a CS Number, which should be refereed to the records of Continuous Service, Series EL and DF (ADM 139 & 188). The series is indexed by ADM 29/97-104, which give either a volume or a CS number. Some of the early volumes also have internal indexes.

Vols	Dates	PRO References
9-10	1834-1835	ADM 29/9-10
15	1834-1836	ADM 29/15
12-14	1835-1837	ADM 29/12-14
16	1837	ADM 29/16
18	1837-1838	ADM 29/18
20-22	1838-1840	ADM 29/20-22
26-32	1840-1845	ADM 29/26-32
35-42	1845-1849	ADM 29/35-42
44-49	1849-1853	ADM 29/44-49
51-96	1853-1894	ADM 29/51-96

Series W

These are entry books kept by the Navy Pay Office of Certificates of Service of warrant officers and ratings sent to Greenwich Hospital to assess the claims of their children for admission to the Hospital Schools. Since orphans had a prior claim, many of the certificates refer to persons already dead at the time of issue. The original certificates will be found in Series EE. The series is indexed by ADM 29/97-104, which gives either a volume or a CS number, the latter to be referred to the Continuous Service records, Series EL and DF (ADM 139 & 188).

Vols	Dates	Remarks	PRO References
17	1836-1838		ADM 29/17
19	1838-1840		ADM 29/19
25	1840-1844		ADM 29/25
34	1844-1848		ADM 29/34
43	1849-1853		ADM 29/43
50	1853-1854		ADM 29/50
	(1855-1857)	*wanting*	
59	1858-1861		ADM 29/59
	(1862-1863)	*wanting*	
70	1864-1870		ADM 29/70
80-96	1871-1894		ADM 29/80-96

Series X

This series consists of Confidential Editions of the *Navy List*, containing the full information included in peacetime editions, but excluded from the wartime edition on sale to the public. Because these Confidential Editions are in a PRO record class they are included here when the peacetime editions are not, but the information they contain is identical. The *Navy Lists* include Seniority and Disposition Lists of all commissioned and warrant officers, including retired and reserve officers in employment, together with yard and civilian officers, WRNS, QARNNS and other Admiralty officials. They are fully indexed.

Dates	PRO References
1914-1918	ADM 177/1-18
1939-1945	ADM 177/19-61

Series Y

These are printed or typescript returns of the marks obtained in examinations by students at the Royal Naval College, Greenwich. They include Lieutenants and Navigating Lieutenants RN, Lieutenants, Captains and Majors RM. There are separate lists for Assistant Engineers (later Engineer Sub-Lieutenants) and Students of Naval Architecture (later Probationer Assistant Constructors). Sub-Lieutenants are included from 1907, and Naval Instructors from 1920.

Dates	Remarks	PRO References
1876-1880		ADM 203/40
1880-1906		ADM 203/21-39
1907-1911		ADM 203/41
(1912-1917)	*wanting*	
1918-1957		ADM 203/42-44

Series Z

These books record the marks obtained in examinations by Naval Cadets in HMS *Britannia*, later the *Britannia* Royal Naval College, Dartmouth. They include assessments of the Cadets' character and abilities, notes of their dates of birth and their parents' addresses. They are arranged chronologically without indexes.

Dates	PRO References
1877-1902	ADM 6/469-473

Series AA

These books record leave given to commissioned officers to live or travel abroad, or to serve in merchant ships, while on half pay. They include Masters, Pursers and Surgeons from 1814. From 1816 the books are arranged in alphabetical order.

Dates	PRO References
1783-1816	ADM 6/207
1816-1847	ADM 6/208-211

Series AB

These are Leave Books recording leave given to commissioned, warrant, Marine and Yard Officers to be absent from their duties. The early books are in alphabetical order within each year; the latter, alphabetical throughout.

Dates	Remarks	PRO References
1804-1836		ADM 6/200-204
(1837-1840)	*wanting*	
1841-1846		ADM 6/205

Series AC

Under a regulation of 1862, married officers were obliged to submit marriage certificates as a condition of entitlement to widow's pensions, and this series represents the surviving certificates, which are clearly only a small proportion of the original total. They cover commissioned officers, including Engineers, Chaplains, Naval Instructors, Marines and officers serving with the Coast guard. Warrant Officers are included from about 1891 only. There is a card index in the PRO Research Enquiries Room to ADM 13/70-71.

Dates of Marriage	PRO References
1806-1861	ADM 13/70
1862-1866	ADM 13/71
1866-1889	ADM 13/186-190
1890-1896	ADM 13/191
1897-1902	ADM 13/192

Series AD

This series consists of papers submitted in support of claims to the Bounty payable to the next of kin of officers and ratings killed in action. They consist mainly of marriage and death certificates, with other documents attesting the age, relationship or poverty of the applicants. There is an index to ADM 106/3021-3034 in the PRO Research Enquiries Room.

Dates	Remarks	PRO References
1675-1684 } 1690-1693 }		ADM 106/3023
(1694-1703)	*wanting*	
1704-1711		ADM 106/3024
(1712-1719)	*wanting*	
1720-1722		ADM 106/3025
(1723-1746)	*wanting*	
1747-1750		ADM 106/3026
1752		ADM 106/3027
(1753-1804)	*wanting*	
1805-1822		ADM 106/3028-3035

Series AE

This series consists of pay lists of the Bounty paid to the widows and dependents of officers, ratings and Marines killed in action. They give the name, address and relation of the payee, the name, quality and ship of the dead man, and the sum paid. There are no indexes.

Dates	*PRO References*
1739-1787	ADM 106/3018-3020

Series AF

These registers were primarily intended as a means of reference to Series EC (ADM 44) but may themselves be used as a summary record of deaths among ratings and Marines, and of the names of their next of kin. The volumes are either in alphabetical order or indexed. The alphabetical order of ADM 141 is an unusual form, in which the order of initial letter is followed by order of the next vowel, and that in turn by the next consonant after the initial letter, whether before or after the vowel. There is some overlap between ADM 141 and ADM 154, but the series is basically the same.

Dates	*PRO References*
1802-1824	ADM 141/1-3
1825-1848	ADM 141/4-6
1849-1861	ADM 141/7-9
1859-1878	ADM 154/1-9

Series AG

These are records of deaths of officers during the 1st World War. The series includes all commissioned and warrant officers and Midshipmen killed or died in service from any cause. The records are on cards, kept in the PRO Research Enquiries Room, which record the name, date, place and cause of death.

Dates	*PRO References*
1914-1920	ADM 242/1-6

Series AH

This series consists of an alphabetical register in four volumes recording the place of burial of all officers and ratings who died from any cause during the 1st World War.

The register gives name, rank or rating, date of birth, date and place of death, name and address of next of kin.

Dates	PRO Reference
1914-1920	ADM 242/7-10

Series AI

This series lists payments of Half Pay to all officers. The early payments are entered in Admiralty Bill Books (ADM 18) which contain many other payments, in no particular order, and are not indexed. The later Half Pay Lists (ADM 25) are in seniority order, and the volumes of PMG 15 either indexed or in alphabetical order. The lists note any periods of employment, dates of death, and leave to reside abroad.

Dates	Remarks	PRO References
1668-1689		ADM 18/44-67
1697-1836		ADM 25/1-255
1836-1838		PMG 15/1-3
1838-1840	Admirals, Captains, Commanders	PMG 15/5
1838-1840	Lieutenants, Chaplains	PMG 15/6
1838-1840	Masters, Surgeons, Pursers	PMG 15/7
1840-1843		PMG 15/9-13
1843-1846		PMG 15/15-19
1846-1849		PMG 15/21-25
1849-1873		PMG 15/27-69
1873-1876		PMG 15/75-78
1876-1879		PMG 15/84-87
1879-1882		PMG 15/93-96
1882-1885		PMG 15/102-105
1885-1888		PMG 15/111-114
1888-1892		PMG 15/120-123
1892-1912		PMG 15/129-148
1912-1920		PMG 15/178-182

Series AJ

These biennial lists were sent by the Admiralty to the Navy Board as authority for paying Half Pay to Flag Officers, Captains and Lieutenants. The dates of any employment, and of deaths, are noted. The lists are in order of seniority and unindexed.

Dates	PRO References
1774-1800	ADM 6/213-219

Series AK

These are internal reports and memoranda of the Victualling Board, then responsible for the naval medical service, concerning Surgeons both individually and collectively, their promotion, pay and conditions. There is much miscellaneous information about named individuals. They are indexed by subject but not by name.

Dates	PRO References
1822-1832	ADM 105/10-19

Series AL

A series of Admiralty Half Pay registers partly duplicating those from the Paymaster-General's department in Series AI. They include Boatswains, Gunners and Carpenters to 1881 only. The volumes are in alphabetical order.

Dates	PRO References
1876-1871	ADM 23/33-34
1871-1881	ADM 23/36-41
1881-1900	ADM 23/125-140
1900-1924	ADM 25/264-276

Series AM

This series combines various payments made by the Admiralty under the authority of Orders in Council. They include superannuation or retirement pensions to Yard Officers and some Captains (from 1666), senior warrant officers (from 1672), senior Lieutenants (from 1737), 'yellow' Admirals (from 1747) and retired Captains (from 1786). From 1673 there are also 'Admiralty' pensions to the widows and dependents of commissioned officers killed in action or in service, and pensions for wounds to commissioned officers. The early payments in Admiralty Bill Books (ADM 18) are mixed with many others. There are no indexes.

Dates	PRO References
1661-1781	ADM 18/39-119
1781-1793	ADM 22/1-5
1793-1821	ADM 22/17-30

Series AN

These are pay books of the Chatham Chest recording pensions paid to warrant officers and ratings disabled by wounds or accidents in service, and to the widows of those killed in service. There are also similar pensions to dockyard employees or their widows.

Dates	PRO References
1675-1779	ADM 82/12-119

Series AO

These volumes are a summary record kept in the Admiralty Office of all salaries and pensions paid by Admiralty order founded on the authority of Orders in Council. They include the salaries of the Commissioners of the Admiralty and Navy and their civil staff. Yard Officers are included, but from 1708 only of minor and overseas yards. There are also 'Admiralty' widows' pensions to the next of kin of commissioned officers (including Marines) and pilots killed in action, pensions for wounds to commissioned officers, Masters, Surgeons and Pursers, and superannuation to warrant officers, 'Yellow' Admirals, some Captains, and Lieutenants. ADM 7/823 is an index to the civil establishment only, excluding pensions to sea officers and their widows. There is a copy in the PRO Research Enquiries Room.

Vols	Dates	PRO References
2	1689-1698	ADM 7/809
1	1698-1721	ADM 7/810
4	1721-1732	ADM 7/811
6	1732-1752	ADM 7/812
7	1752-1763	ADM 7/813
5	1763-1785	ADM 7/814

Series AP

These are the minute books of the Commissioners of the Charity for the Relief of Officers' Widows, recording their decisions on all applications submitted to them. They give the names, often with other information, of all sea officers' widows left in poverty.

Dates	PRO References
1732-1819	ADM 6/332-334

Series AQ

This series consists of the pay books of the Charity for the Relief of Officers' Widows, recording pensions to the poor widows of all sea officers. From 1836 these pensions were charged directly to the Navy Estimates. From 1830 warrant officers warranted from that date were ineligible for widows' pensions, unless killed in service, and did not regain their entitlement until 1864. Engineers' widows received pensions from 1849. All but the earliest volumes are arranged alphabetically.

Dates	PRO References
1734-1835	ADM 22/56-237
1836-1929	ADM 19/1-94

Series AR

These are the papers submitted to the Charity for the Relief of Officers' Widows by officers' widows applying for pensions. They include many marriage and death certificates. There is a card index to the widows' names in the Research Enquiries Room.

Dates	PRO References
1797-1829	ADM 6/335-384

Series AS

This series of papers submitted by officers' widows applying for pensions from the Charity for the Relief of Officers' Widows consists of those doubtful cases which were referred to the Court of Assistants of the Charity for an expert opinion. The papers themselves are similar to those of Series AR.

Dates	PRO References
1808-1830	ADM 6/385-402

Series AT

This series consists of registers of applications made for relief from the Compassionate Fund, established by Parliamentary grant to help dependants (mostly orphans) of commissioned officers (including Masters, Surgeons, Pursers and Marines) not eligible for other assistance. The registers give the officer's rank, date of death, length of service and ship, date and place of marriage, the applicant's age, address, relation to the dead officer and other circumstances. The registers are indexed.

Dates	PRO References
1809-1820	ADM 6/323-324
1820-1827	ADM 6/326
1827-1831	ADM 6/325
1832-1836	ADM 6/237-238

Series AU

These are registers of payments from the Compassionate Fund (later Compassionate List) to dependants (mostly orphans) of commissioned officers killed or died in service. They give the names and ages of the recipients, and their relationship to the dead officers. From 1885 warrant officers' next of kin were eligible.

Dates	PRO References
1809-1836	ADM 22/239-250
1837-1921	PMG 18/1-38

Series AV

These registers were kept in the Navy Pay Office to record the issue to the Navy Office of certificates that pensions had been paid. The pensions are the same 'Admiralty' pensions (at this date known as 'Naval Ordinary Pensions') as in Series AM, that is to say superannuation, pensions for wounds, and 'Admiralty' widows' pensions. From 1825 the volumes are arranged alphabetically.

Dates	PRO References
1818-1826	ADM 22/31-36

Series AW

These registers were kept in the Navy Pay Office to record 'Naval Ordinary' (ie Admiralty) pensions paid by remittance, that is, to persons living at a distance from London, and not employing agents. The pensions are the same as those of Series AV. The volumes are arranged alphabetically.

Dates	PRO References
1828-1832	ADM 22/39-46
1832-1834	ADM 22/50

Series AX

The pensions to the widows and dependants of officers killed in service, formerly paid by the Admiralty under Order in Council (see Series AM) were from 1836 included in the Navy Estimates under Military Pensions Pt. II. They were paid to warrant as well as commissioned officers' widows. The registers also include superannuation for pilots, and from 1857, pensions to holders of the Victoria Cross.

Dates	PRO References
1836-1847	PMG 16/2-5
1848-1870	PMG 16/7-14
1870-1882	PMG 20/1-4
1882-1885	PMG 20/6
1885-1888	PMG 20/8
1888-1891	PMG 20/10
1891-1895	PMG 20/12
1895-1911	PMG 20/17-20
1911-1919	PMG 20/22-23

Series AY

These registers record pensions to civilian officers of the Admiralty and to their widows; including Yard Officers, Commissioners of the Admiralty and Navy, hospital matrons, and Naval Ordnance officers.

Dates	PRO References
1836-1918	PMG 24

Series AZ

These are registers, parallel to those in the Series EV, of retirement pensions paid to Coast Guard officers and ratings, and to the widows and orphans of those killed in service. They are arranged alphabetically.

Dates	PRO References
1857-1935	PMG 23

Series BA

A series of Admiralty registers of officers' widows' pensions parallel to the Paymaster-General's records in Series AQ. They are arranged alphabetically, and include all commissioned and warrant officers' widows' pensions.

Dates	Remarks	PRO References
1836-1839		ADM 23/45-46
(1840-1866)	*wanting*	
1867-1880		ADM 23/47-52
1880-1899		ADM 23/108-123
1899-1932		ADM 23/145-160

Series BB

These are Admiralty registers of officers' children and dependants receiving pensions on the Compassionate List. They are arranged alphabetically.

Dates	Remarks	PRO References
1867-1871		ADM 23/42
(1872)	*wanting*	
1873-1885		ADM 23/43-44
1884-1901		ADM 23/96-100
1902-1926		ADM 23/200-205

Series BC

This is a series of registers kept in the Admiralty parallel to those of the Paymaster-General's Department in Series AX, recording 'Admiralty' pensions to the widows or orphans of officers killed in service.

Dates	Remarks	PRO References
1866-1880		ADM 23/30-32
1880-1899		ADM 23/84-88
1899-1915		ADM 23/161-164
1916-1918		ADM 23/168
(1919-1920)	*wanting*	
1921-1932		ADM 23/169

Series BD

These are pay books of Out-Pensions from Greenwich Hospital, paid to warrant officers, rating and marines not resident in the Hospital. There are notes of men admitted to, or discharged from, the 'House' (ie the Hospital). The volumes are arranged alphabetically.

Dates	*PRO References*
1814-1846	ADM 22/254-443

Series BE

In these registers are recorded the small number of Greenwich Hospital Out-Pensions paid to commissioned officers.

Dates	*Remarks*	*PRO References*
1814		ADM 22/254
1815-1842		ADM 22/47-49
(1843-1845)	*wanting*	
1846-1921		PMG 71

Series BF

From 1836 the pensions for wounds formerly paid by the Admiralty (see Series AM) were (together with warrant officers' superannuation) paid on the Navy Estimates as Military Pensions Pt. I. These registers, kept in the Paymaster-General's Department, record these pensions. Warrant officers and Engineers were eligible for pensions for wounds from 1866; Midshipmen and Naval Cadets from 1902. From 1837 these registers record the Good Service Pensions established in that year to replace the sinecure ranks of General and Colonel of Marines, and like them awarded to flag officers and Captains, and later to civil officers of equivalent rank. There are also special pensions to retired flag officers, of which no more were awarded after 1866.

Dates	*PRO References*
1836-1838	PMG 16/1
1839-1850	PMG 16/3-6
1851-1872	PMG 16/8-15
1872-1920	PMG 16/17-31

Series BG

Greenwich Hospital was abolished in 1869 as an institution accepting In-Pensioners, and some of the funds thus freed were used to establish supplementary pensions paid to deserving commissioned and warrant officers. With these are associated pensions paid from special funds like the Travers, Popeley and Canada Funds, and some pensions to staff of the Hospital and Hospital School.

Dates	Remarks	PRO References
1871-1931		ADM 165/1-6
(1931-1951)	*wanting*	ADM 165/7-8
1951-1961		ADM 165/9

Series BH

These are Admiralty Registers, corresponding to the Paymaster-General's in Series BF, of 'Military Pensions Pt. I', that is to say Good Service Pensions, pensions for wounds, special pensions to retired flag officers (no further awards of which were made from 1866), and pensions to holders of the Victoria Cross, and the Compassionate Allowances to former officers or their dependants ineligible for any other relief, usually because they had been dismissed from the Service.

Dates	Remarks	PRO References
1866-1870		ADM 23/32
1871-1886	wounds excepted	ADM 23/89
(1871-1879)	wounds *wanting*	
1880-1886	wounds only	ADM 23/94
1886-1900		ADM 23/90-93
1916-1928		ADM 23/206-207
1928-1931		ADM 23/144

Series BI

These are certificates of Masters qualifying in seamanship. They give only the fact and date of passing, but are sometimes accompanied by certificates of baptism and service. Since Masters qualified for specific rates of ship, many have several certificates for successively higher rates. The certificates are arranged alphabetically.

Dates	PRO References
1660-1830	ADM 106/2908-2950

Series BJ

These are bound volumes of passing certificates and supporting documents (including baptismal certificates and Certificates of Service) for young gentlemen examined for Lieutenant at the Navy Office, or at home ports. The volumes are approximately in chronological order. There are indexes in the PRO Research Enquiries Room to ADM 107/12-50, and to baptismal certificates found in ADM 107/12-50, and to baptismal certificates found in ADM 107/7 & 12-63.

Dates	PRO References
1691-1832	ADM 107/1-63

Series BK

An incomplete collection of Surgeons' passing certificates from the eighteenth century, issued by the Barber-Surgeons' Company, Surgeons' Hall, or by examining boards of Surgeons at the outports or overseas. They are arranged alphabetically. There is an index in the PRO Research Enquiries Room giving the dates and texts of the certificates, but no references.

Dates	PRO References
c.1700-1796	ADM 106/2952-2963

Series BL

A collection of Gunners' passing certificates from home and abroad. ADM 6/123 is in chronological order, the rest in alphabetical order. ADM 6/128 includes some certificates of service.

Dates	Remarks	PRO References
1731-1748		ADM 6/123-124
(1749-1759)	*wanting*	
1760-1797		ADM 6/125-127
(1798-1802)	*wanting*	
1803-1812		ADM 6/128-129

Series BM

An incomplete collection of original Lieutenants' passing certificates, many of them with supporting documents such as certificates of baptism and service. Up to 1780 they include officers passing abroad. They are bound in alphabetical order for each year.

Dates	PRO References
1744-1819	ADM 6/86-116

Series BN

These registers were kept in the Navy Office to record the results of the examination for Lieutenant. They give name, age, qualifying service, and 'Commissioners'

Remarks' for each candidate. There are some entries of examinations overseas, and some failures. The volumes are in chronological order and not indexed.

Dates	PRO References
1795-1832	ADM 107/64-70

Series BO

These are registers of retirement pensions paid to naval civilian employees, chiefly artificers and labourers in dock and victualling yards and hospital employees, including nurses. There are some widows' pensions to those whose husbands had been killed in service.

Dates	Remarks	PRO References
1830-1837		ADM 23/1-2
(1837-1847)	wanting	
1847-1884	A-Z	ADM 23/3-16
1884-1902	A-Z	ADM 23/56-70
1902-1926	A-Z	ADM 23/108-191

Series BP

A further collection of Lieutenants' passing certificates including some supporting documents. They are in alphabetical order within each year.

Dates	PRO References
1854-1867	ADM 13/88-101
1868-1902	ADM 13/207-236

Series BQ

A series of Engineers' passing certificates, giving the candidates' previous services and age. They are in alphabetical order within each year, and there is an index appended to the class list.

Dates	PRO References
1863-1902	ADM 13/200-205

Series BR

In the nineteenth century it became necessary for Cadets to pass an examination to become Midshipmen. These passing certificates record the candidates' names and marks. They are in alphabetical order within each year.

Dates	PRO References
1857-1866	ADM 13/102
1867-1899	ADM 13/240-245

Series BS

These are passing certificates for Pursers (otherwise Paymasters), giving previous services, but without supporting documents.

Dates	PRO References
1851-1867	ADM 13/79-82
1868-1889	ADM 13/247-248

Series BT

In these ledgers of the Treasurer of the Navy are recorded, among many other payments, bills for Surgeons' pay and 'Free gifts' (an allowance for the purchase of drugs and instruments), and payments to the Barber-Surgeons' Company for surgeons' chests. There is a card index to the names of Surgeons mentioned in these records in the PRO Research Enquiries Room.

Dates	PRO References
1660-1672	ADM 20/1-72

Series BU

These volumes contain the accounts of the Chatham Chest, including receipts of the Chaplains' fourpences (or 'Ministers' Groats') and Surgeons' twopences which were deducted from the Chest's Shillings. They can therefore be used as a source for the names and services of Chaplains and Surgeons. There are MS indexes in the PRO Research Enquiries Room.

Dates	PRO References
1681-1743	ADM 82/3-11

Series BV

These registers of officers' full pay were kept in the Navy Pay Office, later part of the Accountant-General's Department, where they formed the authoritative record of officers' active service, and the source of certificates of service.

Vols	Dates	Remarks	PRO References	Indexes
	1795-1817	Flag Officers	ADM 24/1	internal
1-9	1795-1817	Captains, Commanders	ADM 24/2-10	ADM 24/37-38
1-25	1795-1817	Lieutenants	ADM 24/12-36	ADM 24/37-38
	1805-1814	Sub-Lieutenants	ADM 24/39	
1-11	1795-1817	Masters	ADM 24/40-50	ADM 24/11
1-9	1795-1817	Surgeons	ADM 24/51-59	ADM 24/11
1-5	1795-1817	Assistant Surgeons	ADM 24/60-64	ADM 24/65
1-2	1795-1817	Chaplains	ADM 24/66-67	
1-7	1818-1830	Lieutenants	ADM 24/69-75	ADM 24/76
1-2	1818-1830	Surgeons	ADM 24/77-78	ADM 23/79
1-2	1818-1830	Assistant Surgeons	ADM 24/80-81	ADM 24/82
	1811-1818	Chaplains	ADM 24/83	
	1818-1830	Flag Officers, Masters; *wanting*		
1-4	1804-1820	Captains, Commanders, supplementary	ADM 24/85-88	
1-3	1804-1820	Surgeons, supplementary	ADM 24/90-92	
1-45	1830-1858		ADM 24/93-137	ADM 24/138
1-28	1858-1872		ADM 24/139-168	ADM 24/169-170

Series BW

These are Allotment Declaration Lists returned by ships under the terms of the 1795 Act (see Chapter IV) recording the names of warrant officers and ratings who desired to make monthly allotments from their pay to their wives or mothers. They give the name and quality of the man, name and relationship of the recipient. They are arranged alphabetically by name of ship.

Dates	Remarks	PRO References
1795		ADM 27/1-2
1798		ADM 27/3-6
1802		ADM 27/7-9

(continued)

(continued)

Dates	Remarks	PRO References
1805-1812		ADM 27/10-21
1830-1851		ADM 27/22-113
1837-1852	alterations	ADM 27/114-120

Series BX

These are registers, kept by the Navy Pay Office, of remittances from ships made under the terms of the 1758 and 1795 Navy Acts. They give the name of remitter and payee, the date and sum, and usually the address and relationship of the recipient. Many remittances are to next of kin.

Vols	Dates	Remarks	PRO References	Indexes
1-6	1795-1805		ADM 26/1-6	
7	1803-1805	L-Z	ADM 26/7	ADM 26/21
8-9	1805-1808		ADM 26/8-9	
10	1808-1811	A-K	ADM 26/10	ADM 26/22
11	1808-1811		ADM 26/11	
12-13	1810-1813		ADM 26/12-13	ADM 26/23-24
14	1813-1815	A-K	ADM 26/14	
15	1813-1815	L-Z	ADM 26/15	ADM 26/25
16	1816-1820	A-K	ADM 26/16	ADM 26/26
17	1816-1817	L-Z	ADM 26/17	
16	1818-1820	L-Z	ADM 26/16	ADM 26/26
18	1820-1826		ADM 26/18	
19	1826-1833		ADM 26/19	ADM 26/27
20	1834-1839		ADM 26/20	

Series BY

These are ledgers kept by the Navy Pay Office of Remittance Lists returned by ships paid in home ports, giving the names of payee and recipient. They are indexed by ship only.

Dates	PRO References
1795-1824	ADM 26/28-38

Series BZ

These are Remittance Lists from ships overseas, similar to the Allotment Lists in Series BW, and likewise arranged by name of ship only.

Dates	PRO References
1838-1851	ADM 26/39-54

Series CA

These are ledgers recording payments of full pay to Engineers. Each officer has a page of entries, so that the ledgers have some of the characteristics of a service register. There are two series, of which only Vol. 1 of the first series is indexed.

Vols	Dates	PRO References
1-6	1847-1848 (entries + services)	ADM 22/444-449
1-8	1858-1873 (entries + services)	ADM 22/450-457
9	1871-1873 (entries + services)	ADM 29/113

Series CB

These ledgers record payments of full pay to Boatswains, and closely resemble those Series CA. There are no indexes.

Vols	Dates	PRO References
1-3	1854-1858 (entries + services)	ADM 22/458-460
1-4	1858-1874 (entries + services)	ADM 22/461-464

Series CC

These ledgers record payments of full pay to Carpenters, and closely resemble those of series CA and CB.

Vols	Dates	PRO References
1-2	1853-1858 (entries + services)	ADM 22/465-466
1-2	1858-1874 (entries + services)	ADM 22/467-468

Series CD

A series of Gunners' full pay ledgers, parallel to those in series CA-CC.

Vols	Dates	PRO References
1-3	1854-1858	ADM 22/469-471
1-3	1858-1872	ADM 22/471-474

Series CE

These volumes, originally known as 'Entry Books', record the admission of former ratings and warrant officers as In-Pensioners of Greenwich Hospital. They give the date of each man's entry and discharge. Hospital officers and staff are included.

Dates	Remarks	PRO References	Indexes
1704-1765 (entries)		ADM 73/36 Pt. I	ADM 73/37
1765-1803 (entries)		ADM 73/36 Pt. II	
1765-1812 (entries)	renumbering of	ADM 73/38	ADM 73/39
	ADM 73/36 Pt. II		
1813-1846 (entries)		ADM 73/40	ADM 73/41

Series CF

These 'Rough Entry Books' of In-Pensioners admitted to Greenwich Hospital give more information than those of Series CE, including the pensioner's age, whether married, number if children, birthplace, last residence, trade, last ship, time in service, and whether wounded or ruptured. There are no indexes, but individuals can be located by date of admission using the indexes to Series CE.

Dates	PRO Reference
1704-1863	ADM 73/51-62

Series CG

These registers were kept by the Admiralty to record the names of candidates for admission to Greenwich Hospital as In-Pensioners. They are not entirely consistent in form, but give each man's age, length of service and other claims to favour. The first two volumes only are indexed, and there is a card index to ADM 6/223-247 in the Research Enquiries Room.

Dates	Remarks	PRO References
1737-1763		ADM 6/223-224
(1764-1780)	*wanting*	
1781-1784		ADM 6/225
(1785-1814)	*wanting*	
1815-1859		ADM 6/226-266

Series CH

These registers, known in Greenwich Hospital as 'General Registers of Pensioners and their Families', record each In-Pensioner's age, length of service, nature of disablement if any, ward, whether married, number of children, address of wife, dates of entry and discharge. The first three volumes may represent successive drafts, and are all titled 'Volume I'.

Vols	Dates	PRO References	Indexes
1	1824 (compiled)	ADM 73/42	ADM 73/44
1	1824 (compiled)	ADM 73/43	ADM 73/44
1	1826 (compiled)		
	1779-1833 (entries)	ADM 73/45	
2	1833-1846 (entries)	ADM 73/46	
3	1846-1863 (entries)	ADM 73/47	ADM 73/48
4	1864-1866 (entries)	ADM 73/49	ADM 73/50

Series CI

Those 'Entry Books' of In-Pensioners of Greenwich Hospital give substantially the same information as the registers in Series CH.

Dates	PRO References
1764-1865	ADM 73/65-69

Series CJ

These are pay books of Greenwich Hospital Out-Pensions, giving simply the name of the recipient and the amount of the pension. The signatures of those who drew their pensions in cash appear as a receipt; the letter R against the others stands in this case for 'Remitted'.

Dates	Remarks	Pro References
1781-1801		ADM 73/95-130
(1802-1806)	*wanting*	
1807-1809		ADM 73/131

Series CK

These are minute books, possible of a committee of the Governors of Greenwich Hospital, recording decisions on applications for In- or Out-Pensions or other relief.

The figures in the 'Decision' column represent an annual Out-Pension of so may pounds. Other abbreviations are:

Pr. No:	Pension Number	A:	Admitted
P:	Hospital Pension	CP:	Chatham Chest Pension
R:	Rejected		

The applicants' age, length of service and claims are recorded. There are no indexes.

Dates	PRO References
1789-1859	ADM 6/271-320

Series CL

These records, kept in the Paymaster-General's department, record the payment of superannuation to commissioned officers. These are Naval Ordinary (formerly 'Admiralty') pensions continued from Series AV. The volumes are indexed or arranged alphabetically.

Dates	Remarks	PRO References
1836-1838		PMG 15/1-3
1838-1840	Admirals, Captains, Commanders	PMG 15/5
1838-1840	Lieutenants, Chaplains	PMG 15/6
1838-1840	Masters, Surgeons, Pursers	PMG 15/7
1840-1843		PMG 15/9-13
1843-1846		PMG 15/15-19
1846-1849		PMG 15/21-25
1849-1876		PMG 15/27-73
1876-1879		PMG 15/79-82
1879-1882		PMG 15/88-91
1882-1885		PMG 15/97-100
1885-1888		PMG 15/106-109
1888-1892		PMG 15/115-118
1892-1896		PMG 15/124-127
1896-1912		PMG 15/149-164
1912-1920		PMG 15/170-174

Series CM

The warrant officers' superannuation formerly paid by the Admiralty under Orders in Council (see Series AM) was from 1836 charged to the Navy Estimates under

Military Pensions Pt. I. These pensions were paid to Boatswains, Gunners, Carpenters, until 1874 to Cooks, and until 1877 to Engineers not of commissioned rank. They were payable to Coast Guard warrant officers in respect of service after 1860, and to the new warrant and commissioned warrant ranks from their inception.

Dates	*PRO References*
1836-1838	PMG 16/1
1839-1850	PMG 16/3-6
1851-1872	PMG 16/8-15
1872-1874	PMG 16/17
1974-1924	PMG 69/1-29

Series CN

These registers record superannuation to civilian employees, and run parallel to those in Series BO.

Dates	*PRO References*
1836-1928	PMG 25

Series CO

This series, parallel to Series CM, record warrant officers' superannuation, including the new warrant ranks from their creation. Pensions of Engineers who retired before 1877 without reaching commissioned rank are also included.

Dates	*PRO References*
1867-1871	ADM 23/33-34
1871-1881	ADM 23/36-41
1881-1901	ADM 23/101-105
1901-1031	ADM 23/173-179

Series CP

In this series is recorded retired pay to commissioned officers. The volumes are arranged alphabetically, and give only the officers' names and payments. There is sometimes note of addresses and dates of death.

Dates	*PRO References*
1867-1871	ADM 23/33-34
1871-1881	ADM 23/36-41
1881-1934	ADM 22/488-522

Series CQ

In this series were entered a small number of pensions paid to elderly or disabled officers of Captain's or Commander's rank, and later to Admirals. There are also pensions to former officers of the Ordnance Store Department transferred to the Naval Ordnance Department, and from 1911, pensions to nursing sisters.

Dates	PRO References
1878-1899	ADM 23/83-88
1899-1927	ADM 23/161-167
1927-1932	ADM 23/172

Series CR

These volumes are less a series in the usual sense than a succession of drafts or copies of a list in different forms and brought up to different dates, of all flag officers, Captains and Commanders, with notes of their services, deaths or fates. ADM 10/10 & 15 also include Lieutenants. Some versions are in order of seniority, others alphabetical, and one is a succession book. The original list was almost certainly drawn up by Samuel Pepys, and Pepysian MS 2911 in Magdalene College Cambridge is his own copy.

Dates	Remarks	PRO References
1652-1737	seniority	ADM 7/549
1660-1685	alphabetical	ADM 10/15
1660-1688	alphabetical	ADM 10/10
1673-1754	seniority	ADM 6/424
1688-1725	succession	ADM 7/655
1688-1737	alphabetical	ADM 7/549
1688-1746	seniority	ADM 10/10

Series CS

These service registers of Surgeons were kept in the office of the Physician-General, later Medical Director-General. The series appears to have been begun in about 1825, and discontinued in 1886. It is probable that volume 6 of the Assistant Surgeons' services was then discarded. Although the series is not completely indexed, the cross-references within the volumes as surgeons were promoted from one to another to allow any career to be traced.

Vols	Dates	Remarks	PRO References	Indexes
1	1774-1811 (seniority)	Surgeons	ADM 104/12-13	ADM 104/11
2	1811-1831 (seniority)	Surgeons	ADM 104/14-15	ADM 104/11
3	1831-1854 (seniority)	Surgeons	ADM 104/16-17	ADM 104/11
4	1854-1886 (seniority)	Surgeons	ADM 104/18-19	
1	1795-1827 (seniority)	Assistant Surgeons	ADM 104/20-21	ADM 104/11
2	1827-1839 (seniority)	Assistant Surgeons	ADM 104/22	ADM 104/11
3	1839-1848 (seniority)	Assistant Surgeons	ADM 104/23-24	ADM 104/11
4	1848-1859 (seniority)	Assistant Surgeons	ADM 104/25-26	ADM 104/11
5	1860-1873 (seniority)	Assistant Surgeons	ADM 104/27-28	
6	(1873-1886)	*wanting*		
	1859-1886 (seniority)	Staff/Fleet Surgeons	ADM 104/29	

Series CT

These service registers of Engineers were kept in the office of the Controller of Steam Machinery, later the Engineer in Chief. All the volumes have internal indexes, and ADM 29/131 is an incomplete general index.

Vols	Dates	Remarks	PRO References
1	1837-1839 (entries)		ADM 196/71
2	1839-1847 (entries)		ADM 29/105
3	1839-1853 (entries)	Engineer's Boys	ADM 29/106
4	1847-1854 (entries)		ADM 29/108
5	1834-1846 (entries)	Stokers	ADM 29/107
	1855-1856 (entries)		
6	1856-1859 (entries)		ADM 29/109
7	1859-1862 (entries)		ADM 29/110
8	1862-1879 (entries)		ADM 29/111
9-12		*wanting*	

Series CU

A series of Surgeons' service registers, probably kept by the Commission and Warrant Branch of the Admiralty.

Vols	Dates	Remarks	PRO References	Indexes
1	c.1840-1850	(compiled + entries)	ADM 196/8	internal + ADM 196/26 & 28 (as 'Vol. 1' in *black*)
2	1841-1872	(entries)	ADM 196/9	internal + ADM 196/26 & 28 (as 'Vol.2' in *black*)
3	1872-1895	(entries)	ADM 196/10	ADM 196/27 (as 'vol.3' in *black*) ADM 196/28 (as 'Vol.1' in *red* or 'Vol.1' in *black*)

Series CV

This is the earliest series of officers' service registers, and consists of certificates of service bound up into 'Guard Books' and annotated. They include Admirals, Captains, Commanders and Lieutenants, and in the first volume only, some Masters, Mates, Surgeons, Pursers, and Secretaries. ADM 196/7 is an index to the whole series.

Vols	Dates	PRO References
1-6	c.1843-1875 (compiled)	ADM 196/1-6

Series CW

These service registers were kept in the Commission Branch, and record the entire careers of executive or military commissioned officers entering as Naval Cadets. ADM 196/57 is a complete but not very reliable index to the series.

Vols	Dates	Remarks	PRO References
1	1846-1847 (compiled + entries)		ADM 196/36-37
2	1867-1873 (entries)		ADM 196/38-39

(continued)

(continued)

Vols	Dates	Remarks	PRO References
3	1846-1873 (entries)	Overflow of 1&2	ADM 196/40-41
4	1873-1881 (entries)		ADM 196/42
5	1881-1888 (entries)		ADM 196/43
6	1888-1893 (entries)		ADM 196/44
7	1893-1896 (entries)		ADM 196/45
8	1895-1898 (entries)		ADM 196/46-48
9	1898-1902 (entries)		ADM 196/49-50
10	1902-1905 (entries)		ADM 196/51-52
11	1906-1916 (entries + special promotions & transfers from RNR)		ADM 196/96
12	1903-1904 (entries)		ADM 196/53
13	1905 (entries)		ADM 196/54
14	1905-1906 (entries)		ADM 196/55
15	1907 (entries)		ADM 196/56
16-30		*wanting*	
S	1895-1898 (entries as Lieutenant)	Supplementary List (transferred from RNR) *wanting*	

Series CX

These service registers record the services of Boatswain, Gunners and Carpenters from 1848 to 1855, and of commissioned officers of the civil branch including Masters, from 1848 to 1882, and to death. Only Volume 1 contains Chaplains. The volumes are arranged alphabetically.

Vols	Dates	PRO References
1	1848-1855 (services)	ADM 196/74-76
2	1856-1873 (services)	ADM 196/77-79
3	1873-1882 (entries + services)	ADM 196/80-81

Series CY

This series of registers of service of Surgeons was kept by the Junior Naval Lord as a reference in settling questions of promotion. Much loose correspondence on the merits of individual officers is included. Up to 1874 separate registers were kept for each rank; generally, previous services were copied on promotion, so each book gives complete service up to and including that rank, but not beyond. After 1874 services were, in principle, entered in one book, but in practice many were continued in books of the earlier series. All entries in this series ceased in 1894 except for some notations of deaths. There is no general index to the series, but all volumes are indexed internally.

Vols	Dates	Remarks	PRO References
1	1829-1850 (entries + compiled)	Assistant Surgeons	ADM 104/ 34
2	1851-1860 (entries + compiled)	Assistant Surgeons	ADM 104/ 36
3	1839-1863 (entries)	Assistant Surgeons	ADM 104/ 35
4	1861-1871 (entries)	Assistant Surgeons	ADM 104/ 40
1	1830-1854 (seniority, compiled 1856)	Surgeons	ADM 104/ 31
2	1854-1873 (seniority, compiled 1856)	Surgeons	ADM 104/ 32
	1861-1882 (seniority)	Staff/Fleet Surgeons	ADM 104/ 38
	1861-1887 (seniority)	Deputy Inspectors General	ADM 105/ 75
	1861-1872 (seniority)	Inspectors General	ADM 105/ 75
	1867-1894 (seniority)	Deputy Inspectors General & Inspectors General	ADM 105/ 76
4	1873-1877 (seniority)	Surgeons	ADM 104/ 39
	1864-1887 (entries + services)	all ranks	ADM 104/ 39
5	1871-1878 (entries)	all ranks	ADM 104/ 37

(continued)

(continued)

Vols	Dates	Remarks	PRO References
6	1879-1886 (entries)	all ranks	ADM 104/41
7	1886-1893 (entries)	all ranks	ADM 104/42

Series CZ

These Civil Branch registers of service cover Clerks and Paymasters, Masters and Surgeons (Vol. 4 only), Chaplains and Naval Instructors (Vols. 5-7 only).

Vols	Dates	Remarks	PRO References	Indexes
1	1852-1861 (entries)		ADM 196/11	internal; some in ADM 196/26 & 28 as 'Pay-masters 1'
2	1862-1884 (entries)		ADM 196/12	some in ADM 196/26-28 as 'Paymasters 2'
3		wanting		
4	1881-1891 (entries)		ADM 196/82	ADM 6/442
5	1891-1905 (entries)		ADM 6/443	ADM 6/442
6	1905-1916 (entries)		ADM 6/444	
7	1916-1922 (entries)		ADM 196/85	

Series DA

These are warrant officers' service registers, covering the services of Boatswains, Gunners and Carpenters. There are some Schoolmasters in Vol. 4. ADM 196/33 is an index to the series.

Vols	Dates	Remarks	PRO References
1	1855-1873 (entries)	A-C	ADM 196/29
2	1855-1873 (entries)	D-T	ADM 196/30
3	1855-1873 (entries)	V-Z	ADM 196/31
	1873-1882 (entries)	A-Z	
4	1882-1890 (entries)		ADM 196/32
5		wanting	

Series DB

A series of Engineers' service registers, probably from the Commission and Warrant Branch. They are indexed by ADM 196/26-28, in a rather confusing fashion:

	ADM 196/26	*ADM 196/28*	*ADM 196/27*
Vol. 1:	'1' or 'E1'	'1' or 'E1'	
Vol. 1:		'1' (red)	'1' (black)
Vol. 2:		'2' (black or red)	'2' (black)

Vols	*Dates*	*PRO References*
1	1856-1858 (compiled + entries)	ADM 196/23
1 New Series	1858-1878 (entries)	ADM 196/24
2 NS	1869-1886 (entries)	ADM 196/25

Series DC

A series of service registers of executive commissioned officers giving their entire career from entry as Naval Cadets. It largely overlaps with Series CW. There are three index volumes, ADM 196/26,28 and 27, compiled in that order, of the whole series, each omitting the officers who had died or retired during the currency of its predecessor, and adding new entries, so that none is a complete index to the series. These index volumes refer to several series, and give their references in confusing forms, most simply set out in a table:

Officers	*ADM 196/26*	*ADM 196/28*	*ADM 196/27*	*PRO References*
Lieuts. to Admirals	G.B. 1-6	G.B. 1-6	G.B. 1-6	ADM 196/ 1-6
Mates to Admirals	1-4	1-4	1-4	ADM 196 13-16
Cadets to Admirals	5-7	5-7		ADM 196/ 17-19
		8 (black)/ 1 (red)	1/8	ADM 196/ 20
		2 (red)	2/9	?
			10-16	?
			A & B	?
Supplementary Lieuts.			IR & 2R	?
Masters	1-2	1-2/M1-M2	1-2	ADM 196/ 21-22

(continued)

(continued)

Officers	*ADM 196/26*	*ADM 196/28*	*ADM 196/27*	*PRO References*
Surgeons	1-2	1-2		ADM 196/8-9
	N1/1N	1N/1 (red)	1/3	ADM 196/10
Paymasters	1-2	1-2	1-2	ADM 196/11-12
		3	3-5	?
Engineers	1/E1	1/E1	01	ADM 196/23
		1 (red)	1	ADM 196/24
		2	2	ADM 196/25
			3-4	?
Wt. Officers		1-4/W01-4		ADM 196/29-32
RNR.	7			?
	C.G.1 (red)			?
2nd Masters	M1-M2			?
Chaplains	1	1	1-2	?
	'All Officers'			ADM 196/68
			3	ADM 196/10

Vols	*Dates*	*Remarks*	*PRO References*
1	1861 (compiled)	Lieutenant & above	ADM 196/13
2	1861 (compiled)	Lieutenant & above	ADM 196/14
3	1861 (compiled)	Lieutenant & above	ADM 196/15
4	1861 (compiled)	Lieutenant & above	ADM 196/16
5	1860-1863 (entries)		ADM 196/17
6	1863-1866 (entries)	inc. transfers from Navigating Branch	ADM 196/18
7	1866-1870 (entries)	inc. transfers from Navigating Branch	ADM 196/19
8	1870-1878 (entries)		ADM 196/20
9-16	c.1879-1905 (entries)	*wanting*	

Series DD

These are registers of service of RNR ratings, giving details of their successive engagements in merchant ships as well as their service in the Navy and the usual personal details. The records are arranged in numerical order within each class of ratings, but there appear to be no indexes.

Dates	*PRO References*
1860-1908 (entries)	BT 164

Series DE

These service registers of RNR officers give details of their merchant as well as naval services. They are arranged in numerical order of commission. There are no indexes as such, but ADM 240/13 can be used as an index to Sub-Lieutenants 1-300, ADM 240/14 to 00601-00900, ADM 240/15 to 00901-001200, and ADM 240/31-32 to Engineers 01-0335. Officers' seniority can easily be discovered from the *Navy List*.

Commissions	*Dates*	*PRO References*
Lieutenants 1-275	1862-1890 (seniority)	ADM 240/3
Lieutenants 2-409	1890-1892 (seniority)	ADM 240/4
Lieutenants 410-599	1892-1897 (seniority)	ADM 240/5
Lieutenants 600-797	1897-1901 (seniority)	ADM 240/6
Sub-Lieutenants 1-390	1862-1890 (seniority)	ADM 240/8
Sub-Lieutenants 0011-00536	1890-1891 (seniority)	ADM 240/9
Sub-Lieutenants 00537-00736	1891-1894 (seniority)	ADM 210/10
Sub-Lieutenants 00737-00934	1894-1896 (seniority)	ADM 240/11
Sub-Lieutenants 00935-001134	1896-1897 (seniority)	ADM 240/12
Midshipmen 1-200	1873-1883 (seniority)	ADM 240/19
Midshipmen 201-300	1883-1888 (seniority)	ADM 240/20
Midshipmen 301-503	1888-1892 (seniority)	ADM 204/21
Midshipmen 504-699	1892-1895 (seniority)	ADM 240/22
Midshipmen 700-899	1895-1897 (seniority)	ADM 240/23
Midshipmen 900-1099	1897-1898 (seniority)	ADM 240/24
Senior Engineers 0001-00023	1891-1893 (seniority)	ADM 240/29
Engineers 01-0122	1865-1893 (seniority)	ADM 240/29
Asst. Engineers 001-0049	1865-1893 (seniority)	ADM 240/29
Senior Engineers 00024-00073	1893-1901 (seniority)	ADM 240/30

(continued)

(continued)

Commissions	Dates	PRO References
Engineers 0123-0222	1893-1899 (seniority)	ADM 240/30
Asst. Engineers 0051-00199	1895-1897 (seniority)	ADM 240/30
Senior Engineers 00074-00099	1901-1907 (seniority)	ADM 240/31
Engineers 0223-0296	1899-1902 (seniority)	ADM 240/31
Asst. Engineers 00101-00200	1897-1899 (seniority)	ADM 240/31

Series DF

This is the second series of record rating entering for Continuous Service (succeeding Series EL). It is in a similar but simpler form to officers' service registers. ADM 188/245-267 are complete indexes to the series.

Dates	PRO References
1873-1891 (entries)	ADM 188/5-244

Series DG

These are service registers of Coast Guard Officers, most of whom were RN officers retired or on half pay. The volumes are indexed.

Dates	PRO References
1886-1919 (seniority)	ADM 175/103-107
1919-1947 (seniority)	ADM 175/109-110

Series DH

These 'record cards' are in the form of a summary record of service of each Coast Guard rating. ADM 175/108 is an index to the numbered cards.

Dates	Remarks	PRO References
1900-1923	A-Z	ADM 175/82A-84B
1919-1923	RN Ratings Nos. 112500-358500	ADM 175/85-89
1919-1923	RM	ADM 175/90

Series DI

These two volumes are succession books of inferior officers appointed by Admiralty warrant or order, that is to say Midshipmen Ordinary, Volunteers per Order, Chaplains, Masters at Arms, Schoolmasters and Scholars of the Royal Naval Academy.

Dates	PRO References
1699-1756	ADM 6/427
1757-1824	ADM 6/185

Series DJ

These are succession books of warrant officers other than standing officers, appointed by the Navy Board; that is to say Masters, Surgeons, Surgeon's Mates and Sailmakers. From 1790 they include Caulkers, and from 1799 Ropemakers.

Dates	Remarks	PRO References
1733-1746		ADM 106/2896
1746-1755		ADM 106/2897
(1755-1770)	*wanting*	
1770-1783		ADM 106/2899
1783-1798		ADM 196/2900
1799-1807	no surgeons	ADM 106/2901

Series DK

These are succession books of standing warrant sea officers, that is to say Pursers, Boatswains, Gunners and Carpenters.

Dates	Remarks	PRO References
1764-1784		ADM 106/2898
1785-1799	inc. Yard Officers	ADM 106/2902
1800-1808		ADM 106/2903
1809-1814		ADM 106/2904
1815-1826	inc. Yard Officers	ADM 106/2905
1826-1831	inc. Yard Officers	ADM 106/2906

Series DL

These succession books include Captains, Commanders, Lieutenants, Pursers, Boatswains, Gunners and Carpenters. From 1832 executive officers are in separate volumes and the warrant officers' volumes include Masters, Surgeons, Chaplains, Second Masters and Cooks.

Dates	Remarks	PRO References
1780-1832		ADM 11/65-70

(continued)

(continued)

Dates	Remarks	PRO References
1832-1848	Warrant Officers	ADM 11/71
1832-1847	Commissioned Officers	ADM 11/72

Series DM

These are succession books of Captains, Commanders and Lieutenants, including those holding shore appointments and other miscellaneous employments.

Dates	Remarks	PRO References
1797-1801		ADM 11/56-57
(1802-1805)	wanting	
1806-1848		ADM 11/58-63
1846-1903		ADM 11/73-79

Series DN

These are succession books of the four standing warrant sea officers; Pursers, Boatswains, Gunners and Carpenters.

Dates	PRO References
1800-1812	ADM 6/192
1812-1839	ADM 11/31-33

Series DO

These are succession books of Mates, Midshipmen, Admiralty Midshipmen and Boys 1st Class (later Volunteers 1st Class). From 1821 they include Supernumerary Clerks; from 1830 College Volunteers and College Midshipmen. In 1844 Volunteers 1st Class became Naval Cadets. From 1830 the books also include lists of foreign officers serving in the Royal Navy, and a record in the style of a Black Book of Mates and Midshipmen discharged for misconduct. There is some overlap of dates between the volumes, which are indexed by name of ship and person.

Dates	PRO References
1815-1853	ADM 11/23-30
1853-1888	ADM 11/81-87

Series DP

These Coast Guard records cover both officers and ratings, and are in effect succession books for each Coast Guard station, cruiser or guard ship.

Dates	PRO References
1816-1918	ADM 175/1-73

Series DQ

These are succession books of Master's Assistants and Second Class Volunteers from the establishment of these ranks in 1824.

Dates	PRO References
1824-1829	ADM 6/169
1829-1849	ADM 11/20-21

Series DR

These are succession books in the usual form of Surgeons appointed to ships or to naval hospitals.

Dates	PRO Reference
1870-1924	ADM 104/88-94

Series DS

This series of warrant officers' succession books includes Engineers from 1882 only.

Dates	PRO References	Indexes
1872-1882	ADM 29/125	internal
1882-1892	ADM 29/126-127	ADM 29/128
1892-1896	ADM 29/129-130	internal

Series DT

This survey of the previous services and ages of Boatswains, Gunners and Carpenters in Ordinary, in commission or recently in service was answered by the senior officers of guard ships and dockyards rather that by the men themselves, and includes some assessments of character and health. The returns are numbered but apparently unindexed.

Dates	PRO References
1816-1818	ADM 11/35-37

Series DU

These are returns made by Captains, Commanders and Lieutenants to the 1817 survey of services. ADM 10/2-5 are Sea Officers' Lists annotated to provide indexes. Some stray returns are in ADM 6/66.

Dates	PRO References
1817	ADM 9/2-17

Series DV

These returns were made by Flag Officers, Captains, Commanders, Lieutenants and Masters to a circular of 1822 requiring them to state their ages. In 1831 a supplementary circular was issued to those who had made no return to the earlier survey asking for their ages in 1822. The survey is numbered but no index is known to have survived.

Dates	Remarks	PRO References
1822		ADM 6/73-83
1822	Masters only	ADM 106/3517
1831	Commanders and Lieutenants only	ADM 6/83-85

Series DW

These books, described as 'Sea Officers Lists', in fact contain printed seniority lists only of commissioned officers, including Flag Officers from 1743, Mates and Chaplains from 1844.

Dates	Remarks	PRO References
1717-1846		ADM 118/1-185
1800-1824	duplicates of various years	ADM 118/337-352

Series DX

These are printed seniority lists of Masters. The run is incomplete, and many years are missing.

Dates	PRO References
1780-1781	ADM 118/186-187
1783-1784	ADM 118/188-189

(continued)

(continued)

Dates	PRO References
1791	ADM 118/190
1829	ADM 118/209
1832	ADM 118/210-212
1834	ADM 118/219-220
1836	ADM 118/221
1839	ADM 118/223-225
1841	ADM 118/227-228
1844-1846	ADM 118/183-185

Series DY

These are printed Surgeons' seniority lists. The run is incomplete.

Dates	PRO References
1780-1784	ADM 104/51-55
1787	ADM 104/56
1791	ADM 118/191
1796-1813	ADM 104/57-75
1813	ADM 118/353
1814-1817	ADM 104/76-79
1820-1823	ADM 104/80
1829	ADM 118/209
1832	ADM 118/210-211
1834	ADM 118/219-220
1836	ADM 118/221
1839	ADM 118/223-225
1841-1842	ADM 118-357
1844-1846	ADM 118/183-185
1868	ADM 104/81-84
1878	ADM 104/85
1886	ADM 104/86-87

Series DZ

These are printed Pursers' seniority lists, in a broken series.

Dates	PRO References
1810	ADM 118/192
1812-1822	ADM 118/193-207
1817 & 1820	ADM 118/354-355

(continued)

(continued)

Dates	PRO References
1829	ADM 118/209
1832	ADM 118/210-211
1832	ADM 118/213-215
1832-1834	ADM 118/218-220
1836	ADM 118/221
1839	ADM 118/223-225
1841	ADM 118/227-228
1844-1846	ADM 118/183-185

Series EA

These are surviving fragments of a set of printed seniority lists of Boatswains, Gunners and Carpenters.

Dates	PRO References
1810	ADM 118/192
1812-1815	ADM 118/193-199
1816	ADM 118/201 & 354
1820	ADM 118/205 & 355
1827	ADM 118/208
1833	ADM 118/216-217
1833	ADM 118/356
1836	ADM 118/222
1839	ADM 118/226
1844	ADM 118/229

Series EB

These are original wills of ratings and marines, mostly on printed forms. They are arranged alphabetically and indexed by ADM 142.

Dates	PRO References
1786-1882	ADM 48

Series EC

These Papers contain claims by executors and next of kin for the back pay of ratings who died in service. Some include wills, birth and marriage certificates and other supporting documents, either in original or in copy. They are indexed by ADM 141 (see series AF).

Dates	PRO References
1800-1860	ADM 44

Series ED

These papers concern claims for the back pay of dead officers, and are very similar to those in Series EC. A nominal card index to pieces 1-10 is available in the Research Enquiries Room.

Dates	PRO References
1830-1860	ADM 45

Series EE

These are the original papers submitted in support of applications to enter Greenwich Hospital School. They include certificates of service, baptismal and marriage certificates. The majority concern ratings' children and are not earlier than the nineteenth century. They are arranged alphabetically.

Dates	PRO References
1728-1861	ADM 73/154-389

Series EF

These volumes were known as Registers of Entries and Discharges, but are chiefly concerned with recording when and whither boys were discharged from Greenwich Hospital School, including details of apprenticeship.

Vols	Dates	Remarks	PRO References	Indexes
1	1728-1771		ADM 73/404	ADM 73/438 to 1744
2	1772-1811		ADM 73/405	ADM 73/434
3	1812-1828		ADM 73/406	ADM 73/434
4	1815-1833		ADM 73/412	ADM 73/434
5	1833-1854		ADM 73/413	ADM 73/434
6	1855-1861		ADM 73/414	ADM 73/434
	1728-1786	*duplicate*	ADM 73/416	ADM 73/438 & 434
	1786-1821	*duplicate*	ADM 73/417	ADM 73/434

Series EG

These volumes record 'claimants' (i.e. applicants) for admission to Greenwich Hospital Upper School, giving the boys' names and dates of birth, parents' names and dates of marriage, fathers' ranks or ratings.

Dates	PRO References	Indexes
1832-1844	ADM 73/415	internal
1844-1861	ADM 73/398	ADM 73/ 433
1861-1881	ADM 161/2	internal

Series EH

These volumes record nominations for admission to Greenwich Hospital School (later Upper School) by the Governors (later Directors and Patrons) of the Hospital. They give the boys' names and the patrons'. There are no indexes.

Dates	Remarks	PRO References
1767-1824		ADM 73/407-409
1821-1829		ADM 73/401
(1830-1833)	*wanting*	
1834-1860		ADM 73/ 402-403

Series EI

These volumes record the details of the apprenticeship of boys leaving the Upper School of Greenwich Hospital. They give the boys' names and dates of leaving, and the masters, ships and trades to which they were bound. ADM 73/420 has an internal index.

Dates	PRO References
1802-1870	ADM 73/418-420

Series EJ

These volumes record girl 'claimants' (applicants) for admission to the Royal Naval Asylum (later Greenwich Hospital Lower School). They give similar information to Series EG.

Vols	Dates	PRO References	Indexes
1	1803-1823	ADM 73/391	ADM 73/439
2	1822-1827	ADM 73/392	ADM 73/429

(continued)

(continued)

Vols	Dates	PRO References	Indexes
3	1826-1833	ADM 73/440	ADM 73/430
4	1833-1841	ADM 73/441	ADM 73/444

Series EK

These volumes record boys' applications for admission to the Royal Naval Asylum (Greenwich Hospital Lower School). They give similar information to Series EG and EJ.

Vols	Dates	PRO References	Indexes
1	1803-1823	ADM 73/391	ADM 73/439
2	1822-1827	ADM 73/392	ADM 73/429
3-5	1827-1845	ADM 73/393-395	ADM 73/426-428
6-7	1845-1865	ADM 73/396-397	ADM 73/431-432
8	1865-1870	ADM 161/1	
9-25	1870-1930	ADM 161/3-19	internal

Series EL

This is the first series of Continuous Service records, consisting chiefly of the engagements ratings signed at 18 and subsequent re-engagements, together with a form giving parental consent for those who entered as boys. The class is fully indexed.

Dates	PRO References
1853-1872	ADM 139

Series EM

These particulars of the annual Navy Estimates include lists of officers superannuated up to 1811, and of the recipients of 'Admiralty' widows' pensions and pensions for wounds up to 1818. The lists are closely parallel to those in Series AM and AO.

Dates	PRO References
1708-1811	ADM 181/1-18
1812-1818	ADM 181/19-27

Series EN

These returns were made by Captains, Commanders and Lieutenants to a survey of 1846, requiring them to state their age on 1st January 1846, address, and previous services. Some notes of recommendations are added. ADM 10/6-7 are indexes to the series, and include (black figures) references to returns by Masters to a similar survey of 1851.

Dates	Remarks	PRO References
1846		ADM 9/18-61
1851	Masters only	ADM 11/7-8

Series EO

These are Service Registers of Boatswains. The first volume was compiled about 1860, but shows some services from about 1848. The series includes all Boatswains first warranted from 1860 to 1912, but no services later than 1912. Each volume is indexed. There is some correspondence, chiefly recommendations and testimonials, bound in.

Dates	PRO References
1860-1912	ADM 29/16-119

Series EP

These registers, parallel to those in Series AZ, record civil (as opposed to naval) retirement pensions to Coast Guard officers and ratings, and to the widows and orphans of those killed in service.

Dates	PRO References
1857-1884	ADM 23/17-21
1884-1902	ADM 23/71-75
1902-1926	ADM 23/194-199

Series EQ

These registers record superannuation paid to civil salaried officers in Admiralty employ, including Yard Officers and matrons of hospitals. The registers of Series AY may be used to supply the years missing from this series.

Dates	Remarks	PRO References
1834-1836		ADM 23/25
1836-1866	*wanting*	
1866-1884		ADM 23/26-28
1884-1902		ADM 23/78-82
1902-1910		ADM 23/192-193
1910-1926		ADM 23/196-199

Series ER

From 1842 the Greenwich and Chelsea Hospital Out-Pensions formerly paid by Receivers of Land Tax, Collectors of Customs or Excise, Clerks of the Cheque and the like, were paid by district officers under the authority of the War Office. These returns were made from each district recording statistical and financial information, plus the names of pensioners added by new grant or moving to the district, and deleted by death or moving elsewhere. The returns are complete to 1862, and those for colonial pension districts survive for most dates to 1880, and a few later. There are no nominal indexes.

Dates	PRO References
1842-1883	WO 22

Series ES

These 'List Books' contain monthly lists compiled in the Admiralty showing the station or employment of all ships in commission, with various information about them, including the names of their commanding officers and (to 1808) their Lieutenants. They may therefore be used to trace the careers of these officers, but the lists are arranged geographically, and there are no indexes to officers or ships. There is a copy in the PRO Research Enquiries Room of a manuscript in the National Maritime Museum, consisting of a copy of the typescript *Commissioned Sea Officers List*, 1600-1815 (ed D Bonner Smith & M Lewis, NMM 1955, 3 vols) annotated by the late Cdr Pitcairn-Jones with information chiefly from the List books, which can be used as an epitome or means of reference to them. There are later List Books for the nineteenth century, but from 1815 the genealogical information they contain can more easily and completely be found in the Navy List.

Dates	PRO References
1673-1808	ADM 8/1-95
1808-1813	ADM 8/96-100

Series ET

These service registers record the services of RNAS commissioned and warrant officers while in that service; neither previous RN nor subsequent RAF service is detailed. The volumes are indexed individually, but there is no surviving index to the whole series.

Dates	*PRO References*
1914-1918	ADM 273

Series EU

These volumes were compiled and kept in the First Lord's Private Office for guidance on the promotion of Captains and Flag Officers. They give each officer's services from promotion to Captain only (Vols 1-3 from Lieutenant or Commander), with excerpts or copies of the Confidential Reports on their suitability for flag rank submitted by each officer's Commander-in-Chief. The series was begun in 1901, the first two volumes showing Captains on the Active List of seniority from 1893, and abandoned early in 1944, after which no further annotations were added. Vols 5-8 contain many photographs of the officers concerned. There are no indexes, but as the volumes are in order of seniority in Captain's rank, the *Navy List* can be used as a means of reference.

Vols	*Dates*	*PRO Reference*
1	1893-1895 (seniority)	ADM 196/86
2	1895-1902 (seniority)	ADM 196/87
3	1902-1907 (seniority)	ADM 196/88
4	1907-1914 (seniority)	ADM 196/89
5	1914-1918 (seniority)	ADM 196/90
6	1918-1926 (seniority)	ADM 196/91
7	1926-1935 (seniority)	ADM 196/92
8	1935-1941 (seniority)	ADM 196/93
9	1941-1944 (seniority)	ADM 196/94

Series EV

These medal rolls include both campaign medals, and decorations and awards for gallantry or good service. Most of then consist simply of lists of the names of the officers and ratings concerned, and few are indexed.

Dates	Remarks	PRO References
1793-1840	Naval General Service Medal	ADM 171/1-8
1818-1910	Various campaign medals	ADM 171/9-56
1793-1952	Various medals and awards	ADM 171/57-77
1914-1920	Naval War Medals and honours	ADM 171/89-139
1920-1972	Long Service and Good Conduct Medal	ADM 171/140-163
1942-1972	Various	ADM 171/164-166

Series EW

These 'Honour Sheets' record all recommendations for honours or awards to officers (and a few ratings) during the Great War, together with the results of them and references to the registered papers dealing with the cases. The sheets were organised under letters, which however bear no reference to the officers' names. There is a card index to the names in the Research Enquiries Room.

Dates	PRO References
1914-1919	ADM 171/78-88

Series EX

These registers were kept in the Medical Director-General's office to record the deaths of officers, ratings, Marines, Coastguards, dockyard and victualling yard employees who died from causes other than enemy action. The registers, some of which are closed for seventy-five years, are arranged by ship, unit or establishment, and give the name, rank or rating, date, place and cause of death. There are separate nominal indexes.

Dates	PRO References	Indexes
1893-1939	ADM 104/109-112	ADM 104/102 -105
1940-1943	ADM 104/113-115	ADM 104/106
1944-1945	ADM 104/116-117	ADM 104/107
1946-1950	ADM 104/118-119	ADM 104/108
1951-1956	ADM 104/120-121	internal

Series EY

These registers of casualties are similar to those of Series EX, except that they are arranged alphabetically rather than indexed, and they record deaths by enemy action only. They include Marine other ranks and ratings of the naval reserves, but no commissioned or warrant officers. Some of these registers also are closed for seventy-five years.

Dates	PRO Reference
1900-1941	ADM 104/122-126

Series EZ

These registers record in a single alphabetical series the name, number, rating, ship or unit, date and place of birth, date and category of death of all naval and reserve ratings and Marine other ranks who died from any cause. The 'category' of death is a general classification: 'enemy action', 'missing', 'natural causes' and the like.

Dates	Remarks	PRO References
1939-1948	A-Z	ADM 104/127-139

Series FA

These registers information similar to that in Series EX about officers, ratings and Marines killed or wounded in action. In many cases the person's age is given, and for those wounded, the nature of the wound. The first two volumes are indexed internally by name, the later volumes internally by ship and externally by name.

Dates	PRO References	Indexes
1854-1911	ADM 104/144	internal
1914-1915	ADM 104/145	internal
1915-1929	ADM 104/146-149	ADM 104/140 -143

Series FB

Civil Service Commission examination results for candidates for government employ, including all parts of the armed and civil services. They give the names and marks of both successful and unsuccessful candidates.

Dates	Remarks	PRO References
1886-1991		CSC 10

Series FC

Files of correspondence and papers, forming service registers for WRNS officers. The class list includes a complete nominal list in alphabetical order.

Dates	Remarks	PRO References
1917-1919		ADM 318

Series FD

Termly booklets listing the 'Officers, Masters and Cadets' of RNC Dartmouth. The cadets are listed by term and seniority.

Dates	Remarks	PRO References
1931-1968		ADM 203/104-198

Series FE

Alphabetical registers recording the issue of probate of wills, or letters of administration (for those who died intestate) of RN and army officers and their widows. They give the date of death and an indication of the value of the estate.

Dates	Remarks	PRO References
1836-1914		PMG 50/1-9

APPENDIX III

Naval Reserves and Auxiliary Forces

This is a brief directory of reserves and auxiliary forces raised to assist the Navy up to 1945. It is confined to those which actually entered officers or ratings, and does not include the following:

a)   Operational organisations or formations not recruiting their own personnel (eg Examination Service, Control Service).

b)   The professional specialisation of officers or ratings (eg Meteorological Service, Hydrographic Service)

c)   Entirely civilian bodies in Admiralty employ (eg RN Scientific Service, Admiralty Courier Service)

d)   Indian, dominion or colonial forces.

With these exceptions this list includes all naval forces which were uniformed, subject to naval discipline or engaged in naval operations.

1798-1813 Sea Fencibles
A part-time organisation of fisherman and boatmen, commanded by RN officers, for purposes of local defence, especially against invasion.

1852-1870 Royal Naval Coast Volunteers
A volunteer body whose original structure was similar to that of the Sea Fencibles. When an obligation to serve at sea was imposed, recruiting failed, and the force was eventually absorbed into the Coast Guard.

1857-1923 Coast Guard
In 1857 the Admiralty assumed responsibility for the Coast Guard, which combined several forces of different origins, and different duties. Three distinct bodies need to be noted; the Shore Force, the Permanent Cruiser Force, and the Guard Ships. The Shore Force was a permanent, paid and full-time body of officers and men engaged in a variety of mainly civil functions, but liable to serve afloat in time of war. The Permanent Cruiser Force consisted of the officers and ratings of the Coast Guard (formerly Revenue) Cruisers, which were vessels employed in fishery protection, the suppression of smuggling and other civil duties afloat. Its personnel were likewise employed full-time, and liable for service in the RN in wartime. The Guard Ships were warships in full commission with reduced crews of RN officers and ratings which lay at major ports as headquarters of the Coast Guard districts. Their captains

and senior officers were appointed both to the ship and to the CG district. Once a year the guard ships completed to full complement with coastguardmen and put to sea for training.

In 1919 the Permanent Cruiser force was abandoned and the Shore Force reorganised as a body consisting entirely of naval pensioners. This New Force was transferred to the Board of Trade in 1923. During the Second World War it reverted to Admiralty operational control (but not administration), and with the assistance of the Auxiliary Coast Guard (a part-time volunteer body) was engaged in coast watching, the manning of signal stations, and similar tasks.

1859 Royal Naval Reserve
This was the first specialised naval reserve. It consisted of officers and men actually employed in British sea-going merchant ships, who undertook periodic training.

1874-1891 Royal Naval Artillery Volunteers
A force of volunteers who undertook periodic drill, but were not seamen by profession. It was not viewed with favour by the Admiralty, and never closely integrated with the RN.

1883 Naval Nursing Sisters
There had been nurses in hospitals and hospital ships from the seventeenth century, but in 1854 the Navy ceased to employ women as nurses. In 1883 nursing sisters were re-introduced, with an established organisation. In 1902 this became Queen Alexandra's Royal Naval Nursing Service. From 1898 some nursing sisters served afloat in hospital ships. The nursing sisters were regarded as officers, having authority over sick berth ratings, but until 1977 were not themselves subject to the Naval Discipline Act. In 1982 the QARNNS absorbed the male ratings of the Sick Berth branch.

1883 Royal Corps of Naval Constructors
In its original form this was largely a professional body of the civilian naval architects employed by the Admiralty. It became customary, however, for constructors during their training to serve afloat as Constructor-Lieutenants, officers in uniform, and for more senior constructors to serve afloat when needed, in uniform and ranked as constructor officers. Members of the RCNC therefore serve either as civil servants or naval officers as required.

1891 Naval Ordnance Department
The transfer of responsibility for naval guns from the War Office to the Admiralty required the transfer of various officers of the Ordnance Store Department, who

were employed under special terms and conditions. On retirement they were replaced by RN officers on full pay, or retired and re-employed as civilians. Thereafter the Ordnance Department ceased to present any peculiarities from the point of view of personnel.

1898 Boom Defence Service

There dies no appear ever to have been a formal institution of what became known as the Boom Defence Service, but it may be dated from the introduction in 1898 of Wire Hawser Defence of ports against torpedo-boat attack. In peacetime it was maintained largely by pensioners, in wartime by RNR officers and ratings. The Boom Defence Service was however distinctive in having several ranks and ratings unknown elsewhere in the Navy, such as the Riggers transferred from dockyard employ.

1901-1958 Royal Fleet Reserve

A reserve force consisting of pensioner ratings who had retired from the RN on completion of twenty years' service, but were still of military age. Its equivalent for officers was the Emergency List. In 1958 the RFR was amalgamated with the RNR.

1902 Royal Naval Auxiliary Sick Berth Reserve

A reserve of men volunteering to serve in emergency as Sick Berth Stewards (later Sick Berth Attendants), it was confined to members of the St. John's Ambulance Brigade and the St. Andrew's Ambulance Association Corps.

1903-1958 Royal Naval Volunteer Reserve

A force of officers and ratings undertaking naval training in their spare time, but not professionally employed at sea like the RNR During both world wars the RNVR was the principal means by which officers entered the Navy for the period of the war only, and in 1945 RNVR officers greatly outnumbered those of the RN and RNR together. In 1958 it was amalgamated with the RNR.

1903 Reserve of Medical Officers

This was instituted as part of an unsuccessful scheme to recruit medical officers for short service (four years) followed by a period in reserve. The officers of the RMO promised to serve in wartime, but were not legally bound to, and undertook no naval training.

1910 Reserve of Nurses for Queen Alexandra's Royal Naval Nursing Service

A volunteer reserve of qualified women nurses, who promised to enter (or re-enter) the QARNNS in emergency, but were not legally bound to do so, and undertook no naval training.

1911 Royal Naval Reserve Trawler Section
The RNR as established in 1859 was confined to officers and men of deep-sea merchantmen, but need was appreciated (though vastly underestimated) to employ trawlers in wartime as minesweepers and patrol vessels, and the RNR (T) was set up to enrol the necessary personnel. Though abolished as a distinct section of the RNR in 1921, the RNR (T) or Patrol Service (which was more or less the same thing in an operational form) always remained quite distinct from the RNR proper, and employed the ranks and ratings of fishing boats. In both world wars a very large number of trawlers were taken up by the Navy complete with their crews, who were entered on a form known as T124, by which they were engaged to serve in a named ship for the duration of the war only. Officers and ratings on T124 or similar agreements formed the bulk of the RNR (T) during the First World War.

1911 Royal Fleet Auxiliary
Merchant ships had for centuries been chartered as transports, but difficulties over the legal position of the crew of the hospital ship *Maine*, commissioned in 1902 with a civilian crew, though one of HM ships and part of the Mediterranean Fleet, led to the establishment of a formal organisation of fleet auxiliaries, manned by civilian officers and men in Admiralty employ. Until 1921 the officers were nearly all RNR officers and ranked accordingly; thereafter they were (and are) ranked as other merchant navy officers.

1912-1914 Royal Flying Corps Naval Wing
Some RN and RNVR officers and ratings were attached to the Royal flying Corps, which in its original form was a joint-service organisation, but there was no change in their titles or legal position.

1914-1918 Royal Naval Air Service
This was organised from the RFC Naval Wing, as an integral part of the Navy. Its officers used 'grades' which resembled, but were not equivalent to, those of the RN. Those who held RN or RM commissions or warrants took rank accordingly in the Navy as a whole, while those commissioned from civil life ranked only in the RNAS On the creation of the Royal Air Force in 1918 the officers and ratings of the RNAS either transferred to the RAF or reverted to the RN.

1914-1918 Royal Naval Motor Boat Reserve
This was in effect a detached section of the RNVR consisting of private motor launch owners who manned their own boats and served with the Auxiliary Patrol.

1914-1916 Royal Naval Division

A large number of officers and ratings RNR, RNVR and RFR served ashore in Flanders as infantry. In 1916 the division was transferred to the army as the 63rd (Royal Naval) Division.

1914-1918 Royal Naval Volunteer Reserve Pigeon Service

Pigeons were widely used by aircraft and small vessels, and a small number of pigeon fanciers were recruited into the RNVR specifically to look after them.

1914-1918 Royal Naval Volunteer Reserve Anti-Aircraft Corps

In 1914 the Admiralty was entrusted with the defence of towns and cities against air attack, and the RNVRAAR (sometimes known as the RNASAAC) was established to man guns and searchlights. Its members were either full or part time. In 1916 the air defence of London, and later of some other cities, was transferred to the army.

1914-1921 Shetland Royal Naval Reserve

This was distinct from, and quite unlike the regular RNR, being a coast-watching and local defence organisation similar to the old Sea Fencibles.

1915-1925 RNVR Shore Wireless Service

Instituted as a means of putting under naval discipline, and in uniform, the staffs of Post Office and Marconi Company wireless stations taken over for naval use, it was replaced in 1925 by the SWS.

1916 Royal Naval Transport Service

Transports had been engaged for centuries, usually as chartered merchantmen under the orders of Transport Agents, who were half-pay sea officers employed by the Transport or Navy Boards. A few had been HM Ships manned by RN personnel. The RNTS was an Admiralty organisation to supervise and control (but not man) chartered transports. Its officers (usually retired RN) were uniformed civilian employees of the Admiralty serving afloat or ashore. In 1921 it was re-named the Sea Transport Service and transferred to the Board of Trade, but it remains a uninformed service integrally involved in naval operations.

1917-1921 Army and Navy Canteen Board

Under wartime conditions it became increasingly difficult for commercial contractors to supply naval and army canteens, and the ANCB was established to take their place. In turn it was superseded in 1921 by the Navy, Army and Air Force Institutes. Canteen managers employed by the ANCB and NAAFI served afloat, in uniform and under naval discipline, although civilians and not naval personnel.

1918-1919 and 1939-1996 Women's Royal Naval Service
A uniformed women's service involved in many non-seagoing aspects of naval operation, the WRNS was abolished soon after its first creation, and reformed in 1939. In 1945 a reserve was formed, the WRN(S)R, renamed WRNR in 1947. A peculiarity of the WRNS was until 1977 that its personnel, though naval officers and ratings, were not subject to the Naval Discipline Act.

1925 Shore Signal Service and Shore Wireless Service
These were uniformed, permanent services, manned largely with naval pensioners, which took over duties formerly discharge by the Coast Guard when that organisation was transferred to the Board of Trade.

1932-1938 Royal Naval Wireless Auxiliary Reserve
The RNWAR (sometimes RNAWR) was a body of wireless amateurs who undertook to enter the RN in emergency, but performed no regular training. In 1938 it was replaced by the RNV(W)R, a branch of the RNVR analogous to the RNV(S)R.

1936 Royal Naval Volunteer (Supplementary) Reserve
This was a list of potential officers who offered to serve in the event of war, but (unlike the RNVR) performed no periodic training. Many of its members were yachtsmen or possessed other skills likely to be of use to the Navy.

1939-1945 Royal Naval Patrol Service
In its operational form, the Patrol Service of the Second World War closely resembled that of the First, but the ratings of T124 or similar agreements were entered as RNPS (Hostilities Only). They were liable to serve with their ship wherever she went, but unlike other naval personnel signed a new agreement if they changed ships.

1939-1945 Clyde River Patrol
A force of civilians in naval service, either part or full-time, engaged in local patrol, minewatching and general boatwork in the upper Clyde. There were a number of similar local organisations elsewhere.

1941-1945 Minewatching Service
Early in the Second World War German aircraft began dropping magnetic and acoustic mines in coastal waters. Unlike moored mines, laid by ship in deep water offshore, influence mines were dropped by parachute and lay on the bottom in shallow water. They were impossible to sweep, difficult to counteract, and could only be detected at the moment of dropping. At first on local initiative, later by the Admiralty, an organisation was set up, largely of part-time volunteers, who manned coastal observation posts on moonlit nights to fix the positions of any mines dropped.

The service was disbanded in 1945, but later reformed on a different basis as the Royal Naval Auxiliary Service (RNXS).

1943-1945 Special Repair Ratings (Dockyard)
Established dockyard personnel were obliged to serve overseas if required, but unestablished men, in wartime the larger proportion by far, were not, and it became impossible to man a growing number of overseas dockyards with volunteers and established men alone. No legal provision existed for the compulsory direction of labour outside the United Kingdom, and in order to meet the difficulty dockyard workmen (and a proportion of officers) were conscripted into the Navy as Special Repair Ratings (Dockyard) and ordered overseas. Though uninformed and subject to naval discipline, they were entirely employed on dockyard work. The dockyard officers were ranked as Constructors like RCNC officers.

Officers' Ranks

The majority of these organisations used the ordinary naval ranks and ratings, but some had variations or systems of their own. The following are the unusual officers' ranks; all other ranks either did not exist or did not differ from the RN standards.

Table 8 Unusual Officers' Ranks

Service	Warrant Officer	Sub-Lieutenant/ Ch.Wt. Officer	Lieutenant	Lieutenant Commander	Commander	Captain	Remarks
Coast Guard, Shore Force	Chief Officer	Chief Officer (over 10 years' seniority)	Inspecting Chief Officer, Inspecting Lieutenant, Divisional Officer	Inspecting Lieutenant, Divisional Officer	Inspecting Commander, Divisional Officer	Divisional Captain (1940ff)	Forms of title varied a good deal
Coast Guard, Permanent Cruiser Force	Second Mate (1865)	Acting Second Master (1857) Senior Mate (1865)	Acting Master (1857) Chief Officer (1865)				
Royal Naval Reserve	Warrant Engineer (1903ff)	Chief Warrant Engineer (1916-20)					
Royal Corps of Naval Constructors			Constructor Lieutenant	Constructor Lieutenant-Commander	Constructor Commander	Constructor Captain	When in uniform only, Also in SRR(D), 1943-45.
Boom Defence Service	Boom Skipper (1940) Boom Engineer (1940)	Chief Boom Skipper (1940)					
Royal Naval Reserve (Trawler)	Skipper	Chief Skipper (1916)	Skipper Lieutenant (1935)				
Royal Naval Air Service	Warrant Officer 1st & 2nd Grades	Flight Sub-Lieutenant	Flight Lieutenant	Squadron Commander, Flight Commander	Wing Commander	Wing Captain	Grades, not equivalent ranks
Royal Naval Transport Service (1916)		Transport Officer 4th Grade	Transport Officer 3rd Grade	Transport Officer 2nd Grade	Transport Officer 1st Grade	Deputy Naval Transport Officer	Principal Naval Transport Officer = Commodore
Sea Transport Service (1921)		Sea Transport Officer 4th Grade	Sea Transport Officer 3rd Grade	Sea Transport Officer 2nd Grade	Sea Transport Officer 1st Grade	Deputy Sea Transport Officer	PSTO = Commodore
Women's Royal Naval Service (1918-1919)		Assistant Principal, Quarters Supervisor	Deputy Principal	Deputy Divisional Director, Principal	Deputy Assistant Director, Divisional Director	Assistant Director	Deputy Director = Commodore; Director = Rear-Admiral
Women's Royal Naval Service (1939-96)		3rd Officer	2nd Officer	1st Officer	Chief Officer	Superintendent	

Table of Abbreviations

(Abbreviations used only in Musters and Pay Books are explained in Chapter Four)

ANCB	Army & Navy Canteen Board
Cd.	Commissioned
CG	Coast Guard
C-in-C	Commander- in- Chief
CPO	Chief Petty Officer
CS	Continuous Service
ERA	Engine Room Artificer
GH	Greenwich Hospital
HM	Her Majesty's, His Majesty's
MDG	Medical Director-General (of the Navy)
MS	Manuscript
NAAFI	Navy, Army & Air Force Institutes
PO	Petty Officer
PRO	Public Record Office
PSTO	Principal Sea Transport Officer
QARNNS	Queen Alexandra's Royal Naval Nursing Service
q.v.	which see
RAF	Royal Air Force
RCNC	Royal Corps of Naval Constructors
RFA	Royal Fleet Auxiliary
RFC	Royal Flying Corps
RFR	Royal Fleet Reserve
RM	Royal Marines
RMLI	Royal Marine Light Infantry
RMO	Reserve of Medical Officers
RN	Royal Navy, Royal Naval
RNA	Royal Naval Academy
RNAS	Royal Naval Air Service

RNASAAC	Royal Naval Air Service Anti-Aircraft Corps
RNAWR	Royal Naval Auxiliary Wireless Reserve
RNC	Royal Naval College
RNEC	Royal Naval Engineering College
RNH	Royal Naval Hospital
RNPS	Royal Naval Patrol Service
RNR	Royal Naval Reserve
RNR (T)	Royal Naval Reserve Trawler Section
RNTS	Royal Naval Transport Service
RNVR	Royal Naval Volunteer Reserve
RNVRAAC	Royal Naval Volunteer Reserve Anti-Aircraft Corps
RNV(S)R	Royal Naval Volunteer Supplementary Reserve
RNV(W)R	Royal Naval Volunteer Wireless Reserve
RNWAR	Royal Naval Wireless Auxiliary Reserve
RNXS	Royal Naval Auxiliary Service
SRR(D)	Special Repair Ratings (Dockyards)
SWS	Shore Wireless Service
WRNR	Women's Royal Naval Reserve
WRNS	Women's Royal Naval Service
WRN(S)R	Women's Royal Naval Supplementary Reserve
Wt.	Warrant

Further Reading

Daniel A Baugh: *British Naval Administration in the Age of Walpole* (Princeton, 1965). (Gives a detailed view of eighteenth century naval administration).

Peter Kemp: *The British Sailor* (London 1970). (A brief general history).

Michael Lewis: *England's Sea Officers* (London 1939). (An historical survey; unreliable in detail).

Michael Lewis: *A Social History of the Navy, 1793-1815* (London, 1960). (More accurate than the earlier book; largely concerned with officers).

Michael Lewis: *The Navy in Transition, A Social History 1814-1864* (London, 1965). (Also largely concerned with officers).

Christopher Lloyd: *The British Seaman* (London 1968). (A social history).

N A M Rodger: *The Admiralty* (Lavenham, 1979). (A brief administrative history).

N A M Rodger: *The Wooden World* (London, 1986). ('An anatomy of the Georgian Navy').

David Syrett and R L DiNardo: *The Commissioned Sea Officers of the Royal Navy, 1660-1815* (Navy Records Society Occasional Publications Vol.1, 1994). (An alphabetical list with dates of commissions and other information).

John Wells: *The Royal Navy: An Illustrated Social History 1870-1982* (Stroud, 1994).

Index